# *Primitive*

# A M E R I C A

## *The Ideology of Capitalist Democracy*

## P A U L   S M I T H

University of Minnesota Press

MINNEAPOLIS • LONDON

Parts of the section "imperial power" were previously published in different form in *New Formations* 52 (Spring 2004), edited by Mandy Merck. The section "precarious politics" includes material written as a review article for *symploke* 12, no. 1–2 (2004), edited by Jeff Di Leo.

Published by the University of Minnesota Press
111 Third Avenue South, Suite 290
Minneapolis, MN 55401-2520
http://www.upress.umn.edu

Library of Congress Cataloging-in-Publication Data

Smith, Paul, 1954 Nov. 23–
    Primitive America : the ideology of capitalist democracy / Paul Smith.
        p. cm.
    Includes bibliographical references and index.
    ISBN 978-0-8166-2826-1 (hc : alk. paper) — ISBN 978-0-8166-2827-8
(pb : alk. paper)
    1. Capitalism—United States. 2. Democracy—United States. 3. United States—
Civilization. I. Title. II. Title: Ideology of capitalist democracy.
    HB501.S6364 2007
    973—dc22

                                                              2006033059

Printed in the United States of America on acid-free paper

The University of Minnesota is an equal-opportunity educator and employer.

12 11 10 09 08 07                    10 9 8 7 6 5 4 3 2 1

*Primitive*
# AMERICA

*Dedicated*

*to the memory of*

FRED PFEIL

Now suddenly the West was reduced
to the Paleolithic. We saw that the abstract
was still partly stored in two fragile
standing totems with less resilience even
than Neolithic standing stones.

—JOHN MILBANK (2002)

# Contents

# preamble

erhaps one of the hardest things for observers, local or foreign, to understand about America is the great contrast and massive contradiction between what the anthropologists might call the "hot" and the "cold" elements in the culture. The hot: the dynamic and progressive aspects of a society dedicated to growth and productivity, marked by mobility, invention, innovation, and optimism—in short, a supercharged modernity. The cold: rigid social forms and archaic beliefs, fundamentalism of all kinds, racism and xenophobia, anti-intellectualism, cultural atavism, and ignorance—in short, the primitive. This book is intended to contemplate that contradiction as it is played out in the structure of this exceptional culture.

I see the dialectic between progressive and primitive elements in American culture as a constitutive condition. That is, this dialectic can be located throughout the history of the republic and seen at play in the everyday life and being of the American subject. But as with any dialectical relationship, one side is always in the ascendant, or relatively empowered and facilitated. *Primitive America* tries to make the case that this is one way of understanding the past few tumultuous years since 9/11, and the intricacies of that dialectic are what impel most of the sections of the book. Much of what has happened and that has seemed so egregious or novel to many has in fact deep roots in this dialectic of the hot and the cold, and is in that sense scarcely new or unprecedented. What America is experiencing in itself is the renewed ascendancy of the primitive, and this is what the book tries to look at.

No doubt the term *primitive* will be deemed provocative in some way (particularly to anthropologists, who have spent a few decades trying to extirpate the word from their vocabulary!). Provocative or not, I am using the term as what I hope is an efficient device to highlight the nature of the forces at work in the culture, both historically and in the present. My argument, however, is also that this dialectic is fundamentally authorized and warranted by one other central fact, namely, America's almost complete and unquestioned devotion to the processes of commodification and capital accumulation. If the constitutive feature of modern America is that dialectical play between its "hot," progressive, and modernizing energy and its "cold," archaic, and fundamentalist instincts, what drives this in the end is capitalism itself. I don't quite want to say that there's nothing new under the American sun, but I do want to suggest that anything new has been latent in, or has been prepared by, the fundamental character of capitalism as it has developed in and shaped this peculiar republic.

America's more or less absolute devotion to the fundamental propositions and processes of its own historical form of capitalism becomes, in my argument, its quintessentially primitive characteristic. This is the book's broadest thematic and I track it by way of a number of other themes that I hope touch on the most important aspects of the structuring of the culture. Approximately the first half of the book tries to lay out what I understand to be the idea of the primitive, dealing with issues such as the history of primitive accumulation, commodity fetishism, the narcissistic inflection of the subject, and the production of American mythographies and atavism. The remainder of the work tracks some of the symptoms of the primitive as I think they appear in the current conjuncture, and thus I deal with issues such as the nature of U.S. imperialism, the state of the law in relation to the Constitution or human rights, and so on.

Many of the symptoms of the primitive that I track have come into especial prominence in the years since the terrorist attacks of September 11, 2001, and it goes without saying that the sheer fact of 9/11 is inescapable. But I want to stress that *Primitive America* is not *about* 9/11, and may indeed be more about the violence that 9/11 provoked. While the immediate, affective shock of the terrorist attacks has probably receded for most Americans, their consequences and effects continue around the globe. In particular, the few square miles of Washington, D.C., have become the epicenter of global control over a formidable conflict. What is now officially known as "The Long War" is being conducted against an indistinct enemy whose threat has been parlayed into something beyond that of even the Soviet Union in the cold war. The Pentagon's 2006 *Quadrennial Defense Review* suggested that this "war" against "violent extremists" is "unprecedented in its complexity." This "Long War" is, in my view, more significant than 9/11 itself and will have more far-reaching consequences.

And yet, in 2006, as America once again reconfigured its massive military machine to face the threat, very few Americans took the time to ask: "America's enemies may be ruthless, but are they really trying to destroy its way of life? Are Osama bin Laden and Co. truly on the same level as Hitler or Stalin?" (*The Guardian,* February 15, 2006). Instead, the course had been set. Five years after an event whose death toll has since been dwarfed many times over not by any act of terrorism but by natural disasters, the AIDS epidemic, structural poverty around the globe, and of course by American military action, the United States geared itself up to hone its "speed, agility, precision and lethality in force" (*Quadrennial Defense Review*).

The harsh realities of the Long War do, of course, occasionally impinge on the consciousness of Americans, particularly those aspects that pertain to the occupation of Iraq. But the Long War is by and large now just a given for most Americans, demanding not much more from them than new levels of patience in the lines at airport security. But in its determination to conduct this Long War, the Bush administration has often called on the events of 9/11 to secure the public's general acceptance (even of the Iraq invasion, which had little or nothing to do with 9/11). The fact of 9/11 not only pervades the words of the current administration, fueling its extraordinary military spending and scarifying budget deficits, but it runs through the everyday life and culture of the nation. The event constitutes an indelible backdrop to the discourses of the media and the administration, and has sat as a kind of eerie presence in the culture over the past five years.

Obviously, during those five years much ink (both real and digital)

has been spilled in an attempt to grapple with the event itself, as well
as the U.S. response and its effects and consequences. *Primitive America*
does not pretend to add much to the kind of discussion that simply
debates the rights and wrongs of the Bush administration's response. In
other words, this book is not intended to join the lists as yet another
anti-Bush screed. There have been many of those—and no doubt there
is room and justification for many more. Indeed, as far as I'm concerned, the post–9/11 posture and behavior of the Bush administration
equal or exceed the misdoings of any administration I can think of in
the blood-spattered and criminal annals of the republic. And this administration has, moreover, been egregious for the brazenness of its
malfeasance, and remarkable for the aura of impunity and the lack of
accountability that seem to surround and protect it.

But put simply, the issues this book addresses are broader than the
actions and ideologies of the Bush administration in the past few years.
I'm more concerned with what might be called the underlying structure of the republic, and with some of the processes—historical and
contemporary—whereby the post–9/11 farrago becomes possible. In
other words, if I am trying to add to an understanding of the apparent
peculiarity of the past few years, it is only by asking how they have been
prepared by or been latent in some of the discernible patterns and features of America and its history.

At the most general level, I take my watchword from one of the
several almost forgotten commentators on America who are featured in
this book: Johan Huizinga bluntly proposed, more than eighty years
ago, that "every political or cultural question in America is an economic
one" (9), and I take this seriously. This means that my principal emphasis is one that scarcely appears in mainstream discourses and discussions—an emphasis that one might even claim is generally proscribed.
America has given itself over so thoroughly to the workings of its peculiar kind of capitalism that it sometimes seems as if nothing else can
be imagined or even spoken of. For the corporate media in this country,
for instance, the economic is reduced to the technical realm of economic management, largely extrinsic to the processes of politics and
culture. Just as distressing perhaps, and as I show later in the book,
even the putatively oppositional discourse of the liberal intelligentsia is

chronically unwilling to tackle or challenge the regime of capital accumulation that dictates America's course. So, my task has been to inquire, in essence, what happens to an understanding of the condition in which this peculiar republic now finds itself if one maintains and insists on the crucial factor of the politico-economic structures and formations of this nation—its primitive and fundamental formations.

## "we" and "you"

> The reaction to the events of 11 September—
> terrible as they were—seems excessive to
> outsiders, and we have to say this to our
> American friends, although they have become
> touchy and ready to break off relations with
> accusations of hard-heartedness.
>
> —Doris Lessing

oris Lessing's rueful but carefully aimed words (published in a post–9/11 issue of *Granta* magazine, where a constellation of writers had been asked to address "What We Think of America") have obviously done little to inhibit the progress of American excess in the five years since the terrorist attacks. In the immediate aftermath of the attacks, the voices of even the most considerable of foreign intellects were hardly alone in being rendered inaudible by the solipsistic noise that immediately took over the American public sphere. All kinds of voices and words, from within America and without, immediately lost standing and forfeited the chance to be heard, became marginalized or simply silenced, in the face of a media-led straitening of the possible range of things that could be said. And even after the initial shock of 9/11 had receded, one's standing to speak depended largely on the proximity of one's sentiments to the bellicose sound bites of the American president as his administration set sail for retaliatory and preemptive violence and as he promoted a Manichaean worldview where one could be only either uncomplicatedly for or uncomplicatedly against America, even as it conducted an illegal, immoral, and opportunistic war.

The peculiar American reaction to 9/11 was always latent in the discursive and cultural habits of this society where, as Lessing pointedly insists, "everything is taken to extremes." Such extremism is perhaps not often enough considered, she suggests, when one tries to understand or account for the culture (54). I'm not sure that it's the case that American extremism has exactly gone unnoticed; it is, after all, the motor and at the same time the effect of the sheer quotidian brutality of American social relations. But the sudden shock to the American system delivered by the terrorists certainly facilitated a renewed kind of extremism, a new and improved brand of extreme Americanism.

That extremist Americanism is foundational to this culture. In his book, *America* (1988), Jean Baudrillard has proposed that the country is "the only remaining primitive society . . . a utopia that is in the process of outstripping its own moral, social and ecological rationale" (7). And this is, moreover, a primitivism awash with its own peculiar set of fundamentalisms—not quite the fundamentalisms that America attacks elsewhere in a kind of narcissistic rage, but fundamentalisms that are every bit as obstinate. The United States of America is, after all, a society where public discourse regularly pays obeisance to ancient texts and their authors, to the bible of personal and collective therapy, to primitive codes of morality and moral equivalency, and so on. And this is to leave aside the various Christian and populist fundamentalisms, influences on the public sphere that have always been present, but which have become more visible in the years since 9/11.

But its most respectable—and indeed, mostly unchallenged—fundamentalism is the deep devotion to the processes of an extreme capitalist economy and to all its attendant social and cultural appurtenances. This has always been the most important fundamentalism of the United States, ever since the founding fathers confirmed their determination that Americans would be a commercial people; and in the era of globalization this has become an even more self-evident and unavoidable fundamentalism. Thus America is a primitive society in a politico-economic sense, too: a society completely devoted to the upkeep of its particular means of production and consumption, and thus deeply dependent on the class effects of that system and ideologically dependent on ancient authorities, which remain tutelary and furnish the ethical life of the culture.

It is to these kinds of fundamentalism that America reflexively appealed after 9/11, by way of phrases such as "our values," "who we are," "the American way of life," and so on; or when New York's Mayor Rudy Giuliani and others explicitly promoted economic consumption as a way of showing support for America. None of that was perhaps terribly surprising, however disturbingly crass it might have been, and it quickly became clear how much it was necessary for the production of the forthcoming war economy in the United States. But the construction of such extremist platitudes (endlessly mediatized, to be sure) was surprisingly successful in effecting the elision of other kinds of speech in this nation, where the idea of freedom of speech is otherwise ideologically canonized as a basic and supposedly inalienable right.

But (as Alexis de Tocqueville was always fond of repeating) this is also a nation where dissidents quickly become pariahs and strangers. The voices and the kinds and forms of speech that were silenced or elided in the aftermath of 9/11 are, of course, the dialectical underbelly to the consolidation of a fundamentalist sense of America, and to the production of an excessive cultural ideology of shared values. They go some way to constituting, for the sake of what I have to say here, a "we"—strangers both within the land and beyond it. This is not, of course, a consistent "we," readily located either beyond or within the borders of the United States and who could be called on to love or hate or to love/hate some cohesive "you" that until recently sat safely ensconced inside those same borders. It goes without saying that nobody within or without those boundaries can be called on *individually* to comply seamlessly, or closely, or for very long, with a discourse of putative national identity. So in the end there is no living "you" or "we" here, but only a vast range of disparate and multifarious individuals, living in history and in their own histories, imperfectly coincident with the discursive structure of "America."

And yet imaginary relations are powerful, perpetually forming and reforming the subjects that are caught up in them. The "you" whose sense of belonging to, or owning, that fundamentalist discourse has for the past five years asserted or constructed itself qua America; and the construction appeared to have been buttressed by the results of the 2004 election. But it is, of course, still unclear who "you" really are. It has never been clear to what extent a "you" could be constructed on the ground by way of ideological and mediatized pressure. It's certainly unclear how much the mainstream surveys could tell us, conducted as they are through the familiar corporate, university, and media channels. And it would be grossly simplistic to try to "read" the nation's ideology through its mediatized messages and simply deduce that people believe (in) them. This is what's wrong with the kind of reading of American ideology that is often produced outside of America, such as the post-9/11 book, *Why Do People Hate America?* (2002) by Ziauddin Sardar and Merryl Wyn Davies, where an absolute coincidence is assumed between media and ideological messages and what people actually believe or think. Or again, the British *Daily Mirror* headline on the morning after the 2004 election—"How Can 59,054,087 People Be So DUMB?"—misses the point by imagining some straightforward correlation between a whole set of ideological imperatives and the votes of individual persons.

So the question of "who are 'you'?" remains opaque in some way. At the same time, there *is* some sort of discursive space where the every-day people that American subjects are coincide with the "you" that is now being promulgated as fundamental America.

But by the same token, there is also some kind of "we" that derives from the fact that the identities and the everyday lives of so many out-side the United States are bound up with the United States, with what the United States does and says, and with what it stands for and fights for. The ways in which "our" identities are thus bound up are different for some than for others, obviously, and "we" are all in any case different from one another. I share nothing significant, I think, with the perpe-trators of the attacks on the World Trade Center (WTC), nor with those British subjects who attacked London in 2005. But some of "us" find ourselves actually inside the boundaries of the United States. That's where I speak from right now, a British subject, but one whose adult life has been shaped by being an alien inside America and thus to some large extent shaped by "you"—and certainly dependent on "you" in all kinds of ways. And there are many in similar positions: some were killed in the WTC attacks, others are Muslims, others illegals, and so on—and none of them is the self-evident other who is targeted in Iraq or Afghanistan, captured and rendered for torture in various nations, or simply detained indefinitely in Guantánamo Bay or in one of America's other prisons around the world. And then there are, of course, also the internal "dissenters"—those who manage to speak and somehow find ways to be heard outside—and occasionally inside—the channels that promote the construction of a "you." All of "us," then, inside and out-side the borders of the United States, are not "you"—a fact that "you" make clear enough on a daily basis.

# dialectics

he American "we" is, in fact, a construct of the very "you" I have just been talking about. This "we" is generated through the power of the long, blank gaze emanating from the American republic that dispassionately, without empathy, and certainly without love, refuses to recognize most of the features of the world laid out at its feet; a gaze that can acknowledge only that part of the world that is compliant and willing to act as a reservoir of narcissistic supply to the colossus.

Appropriately (in light of the events of 9/11, certainly, and probably before that), it is to the World Trade Center that Michel de Certeau pointed when he wanted to describe the ideological imposition that such a gaze exerts over the inhabitants of a given space. In his famous essay, "Walking in the City" (1984), he begins his disquisition from the 110th floor of the World Trade Center, meditating on the ichnographic gaze that the tower (then) enabled, looking down over a city that becomes for him a "texturology" of extremism, "a gigantic rhetoric of excess in both expenditure and production" (91)—and, he might have added, of consumption. That gaze is for him essentially the exercise of a systematic power, or a structure in other words. Its subjects are the masses in the streets, all jerry-building their own relation to that structure as they bustle and move around the spaces of this excessive city.

De Certeau doesn't say so exactly, but one could suspect that he reads the tower and the view it provides by reference to the mystical eye sitting atop the pyramid on the United States' republican seal and, of course, on the dollar bill—another essential trope in America's primitive discourse, the god who oversees "your" beginnings (*Annuit Coeptis*). At any rate, it's hard not to be struck in his account by the way the relationship between the systematic ichnographic gaze and the people scurrying below replicates a much more Hegelian dialectic: the master-slave dialectic. De Certeau's sense of power relations never quite manages to rid itself of that Hegelian, or even Marxist, sense that the grids of power here are *structural* rather than untidily organic in some more Foucauldian sense. The gaze he interprets is in that sense the colossal gaze of the master, surveying the slaves. It is the gaze of a "you" for whom the real people, foraging below and finding their peculiar ways of living within the ichnographic grids that are established for them, can be seen only as subjects, and discerned only according to the degrees of their conformity. And when the structure itself feels threatened by the agitation and even the independence of the subjects under its sway (as, in de Certeau's analysis, the city structure begins to decay and its hold on the city dwellers is mitigated), it tries to gather them in again by way of narratives of catastrophe and panic (96).

One boon of the 9/11 attacks for the colossus was, of course, the opportunity to legitimize such narratives. And the habit of propagating and disseminating such narratives has been a feature of the Bush administration ever since: from the questionable deployment of security alerts after 9/11, through the 2004 election campaign and the casting of doubt on John Kerry's ability to keep the country safe, up to the present, with the administration's repeated insistence that "we" are not safe, and the multifarious attempts to frighten the American people on topics ranging from terrorism to Social Security.

I cite de Certeau's dense essay in part because it has been strangely absent from the many efforts of sociological and cultural studies to "reimagine" New York after 9/11; one might have thought that a text as important as this one could have something to teach us about the intersections of power and control in a modern city. But I cite it more for the reminder it offers—coincidentally beginning from the same place, as it were, as the terrorist attacks themselves—of the way that the spatial structure of the city "serves as a totalizing and almost mythical landmark for socioeconomic and political strategies." Part of the lesson of this conceit is the knowledge that in the end, the city is "impossible to administer" because of the "contradictory movements that counterbalance and combine themselves outside the reach of panoptic power" (95). De Certeau's New York City and its power grid act as a reasonable metaphor for the way in which "our" identities are variously but considerably construed in relation to "you." "Your" identity is the master's identity in which "we" dialectically and necessarily find "our" own image, "our" reflection, and "our" identity. The master's identity is *inflected* to the solipsism of self-involvement and entitlement while emanating its own narcissism and haughty indifference toward "us." At the same time, "we" marginally escape, causing small disturbances and ragged flaws in the ichnographic field.

The situation is familiar, then. In the places, histories, and structures that "we" know about, but of which "you" always contrive to be ignorant, it is a situation historically marked by the production of antagonism and ressentiment. What the master cannot see in the slave's identity and practice is the empirical fact that ressentiment doesn't derive from envy or covetousness, or from a generalized lack of intelligence or understanding, or from any irreconcilable cultural difference or antagonism, and still less from any condition of pure evil. Rather, it derives from a sense of injustice, a sense of being ignored, marginalized, disenfranchised, and undifferentiated. That sort of sense of injustice can only be thickened in relation to an America whose extremist view of itself depends on the very image of freedom, equality, and democracy that the slave necessarily aspires to. Ressentiment in that sense derives from the ever-growing sense of horror that the master cannot live up to the very ideals he preaches to "us." That sensation has been vindicated many times over in the past, and more recently it seemed further confirmed by George Bush's 2004 inauguration speech, in which his call for freedom from tyranny around the world clashed with the continuing narratives of America's own tyrannical and unabashed disregard for the freedom of others; or by the obvious discomfort caused by the democratic election of Hugo Chavez and Evo Morales in Latin America and, even more, of Hamas in Palestine.

Jean Baudrillard, in his idiosyncratic (but nonetheless correct) way, installs this ressentiment at the very heart of his short, yet I think profound, analysis of the events of 9/11, *The Spirit of Terrorism* (2002). Whatever else can be located in the way of motivation for those attacks, he suggests, they represented an uncomplicated form of ressentiment whose "acting-out is never very far away, the impulse to reject any system growing all the stronger as it approaches perfection or omnipotence" (7). Moreover, Baudrillard is equally clear about the problem with the "system" that was being attacked: "It was the system itself which created the objective conditions for this retaliation. By seizing all the cards for itself, it forced the Other to change the rules" (9). In a more prosaic manner, in *9-11* (2001) Noam Chomsky notes something similar in relation to the attacks when he says that they marked a form of conflict qualitatively different from anything America had seen before, not so much because of the scale of the slaughter, but more simply because America itself was the target: "For the first time the guns have been directed the other way" (11–12). Even in the craven and largely "embedded" mainstream American media there was a glimmer of understanding about what was happening; the word *blowback,* a piece of CIA vocabulary that floated around for a while (courtesy of Chalmers Johnson's 2000 book of the same name), could be understood as a euphemism for this new stage in a master/slave narrative.

As the climate in America since 9/11 has shown very clearly, such thoughts are considered unhelpful for the construction of a "you" that could support a state of perpetual war, and noxious to the narratives of catastrophe and panic that have been put into play to round up the faithful. The notion, in any case, that ressentiment is not simply reaction, but a necessary component of the master's identity and history, would always be hard to sell to a "you" that narcissistically cleaves to what Arvind Rajagopal calls "the impossible desire to be both omnipotent and blameless" (175). The United States has been chronically unable to process the ressentiment of the rest of "us," blocking it with vetoes and jet fighters, or with coups and dollars, preventing it from being played out in public spaces and the media, and essentially turning it into the festering wound of antagonism that Nietzsche memorably spoke about. Far from recognizing that festering wound, this is a nation, after all, that has been chronically hesitant to face up to ressentiment in its *own* history, and mostly able to ignore and elide the central antagonisms of class that are produced by its primitive dedication to capitalist social relations. This is and has been a self-avowed "classless" society, *unable therefore to acknowledge its own fundamental structure,* its own fundamental(ist) economic process (except as a process whereby some of its subjects fail to emulate the ability of some of the others to take proper advantage of a supposedly level playing field, or of the fantasized equality of opportunity in America).

For many of "us," it has always been and it remains hard to comprehend how most Americans manage to live in ignorance of class and to maintain ignorance of their own individual relationship to capital's circuits of production and consumption. It's difficult to understand, at least, how such ignorance can survive the brutal empirical realities of America today. The difficulty was by no means eased when it became known that families of 9/11 victims would be paid compensation according to their relatives' value as labor, and that this somehow seemed an unexceptionable arrangement to "you." And the Bush administration's callous evaluation of the lives of African Americans in the wake of Hurricane Katrina, while it outraged the mainstream media for a while, has so far gone unpunished. Indeed, one of the principal conclusions that many drew from what Katrina had exposed—the fragility and impoverishment of the lives of America's working class, particularly its African American citizenry—failed to move the Bush administration. Katrina and the rebuilding of the region around New Orleans had barely receded from the headlines before Bush's 2006 budget proposed further and deeper cuts in spending that would immediately worsen the plight of the country's poor. The blindness of the colossal gaze as it looks on even America itself is replicated in the gaze outward as it looks on "us." This is a nation largely unseeing and closed off to the very conditions of its own existence—a nation blindly staring past history itself.

"Events are the real dialectics of history," Gramsci says, "decisive moments in the painful and bloody development of mankind" (1990, 15), and 9/11, the only digitized date in world history, can be considered an event that might even yet be decisive. It would be tempting, of course, to say that once the "end of history" had supposedly abolished all Hegelian dialectics—wherein "our" identities would be bound up with "yours" in an optical chiasmus of history—it was inevitable that history itself should somehow return to haunt such willed and sanctified ignorance of historical conditions. Yet, from 9/11 onward, through the occupation of Iraq and the identification of a foreign "axis of evil," through the 2004 election and the identification of new "outposts of tyranny," and up to the 2006 confrontations with Iran and support for Israel's attempts to eradicate Hezbollah, the nation appears determined to remain *ex-historical*. It seems, that is, perpetually unable to recognize itself in the face of the other—and that has always made magisterial violence all the more likely (and no doubt will again).

# freedom, equality, democracy

If this dialectic between the "you" and the "we" can claim to represent anything about America's *outward* constitution, it would necessarily find some dialectical counterpart in the *inward* constitution of this state. At the core of the fundamental notions of "the American way of life" that "you" rallied around after 9/11, that allow "you" to kill Iraqis in order to liberate them, and that appear daily in governmental and media discourses, there are several pivotal terms. These are the heavily freighted notions of freedom, equality, and democracy that, more than a century and a half ago, de Tocqueville deployed as the central motifs of *Democracy in America* (1835). De Tocqueville's central project is hardly akin to my project here, but it wouldn't be far-fetched to say that his work does, in fact, wage a particular kind of dialectical campaign. That is, *Democracy in America* plots the interaction of the terms *freedom* and *equality* in the context of the new American republic, which he thought could be a model for Europe's emerging democracies.

De Tocqueville's analysis of how freedom, equality, and democratic institutions interact with (and, indeed, interfere with) one another still remains a touchstone for understanding the peculiar blindnesses that characterize America today. One of its main but largely under-appreciated advantages is that it makes clear that freedom, equality, and democracy are by no means equivalent to each other—and one might even say, they are not even preconditions for one another, however much they have become synonyms in "your" vernacular. While de Tocqueville openly admires the way America instantiates those concepts, he is endlessly fascinated by the untidiness and uncertainty of their interplay. That interplay entails the brute realities of everyday life in a culture marked for him by a unique dialectic of civility and barbarity. In the final analysis, de Tocqueville remains deeply ambivalent about the state of that dialectic in America, and thus remains unsure about the nature and future of the civil life of America as it sustains its peculiar symbiosis of the sophisticated and the primitive.

Unsurprisingly, de Tocqueville's ambivalence ultimately devolves into the chronic political problem of the relationship of the individual to the state. One of the effects of freedom and equality, he suggests, is the increasing ambit of state functions and an increasing willingness on the part of subjects to allow a widening of that influence. This effect is severe enough to provoke de Tocqueville to rather extreme accounts of it. For example, his explanation of why ordinary citizens seem so fond of building numerous odd monuments to insignificant characters is that this is their response to the feeling that "the individual is nothing but the state is limitless" (443). His anxiety about the strength of such feelings is apparent when he discusses the tendency of Americans to elect what he calls "tutelary" government: "They feel the need to be led and the wish to remain free" and they "leave their dependence [on the state] for a moment to indicate their master, and then reenter it" (664).

This dependent tendency derives, he says, from "equality of conditions" in American life. In the immense literature on de Tocqueville's influential ideas, it is shocking how infrequently that basic proposition about America has been challenged. But, as Michael Denning has pointed out, although de Tocqueville's thesis about the equality of conditions is his "master concept," nonetheless "his account of those conditions is simply wrong" (198–99). Equality of rights, education, and economic opportunity did not exist in nineteenth-century America, with its social, political, cultural, and economic divisions based on property, race, and gender. De Tocqueville's claim about equality of condition essentially constitutes an ideological acceptance of a tenet that has underpinned and continues to underpin the condition of the American "you." That is, one of the fundamental building blocks of America's extreme capitalism is what I have called elsewhere, and will discuss a little later, the "subject of value"—a subject whose belief in and acceptance of the principle of equality is required, even in the face of contradictory empirical evidence. This subject of value in capitalism operates from the base of a self-interested rationality, is convinced of the existence and efficacy of equality, and accepts the principle of private property in all realms of social and cultural life.

One principal effect of these conditions is the elision of the empirical realities of class and class interests. But equally, the establishment of the subject of value helps inform the subject's relation to the state, and a view of the state as the proper and delimited locus of political power. That is, the belief in equality of conditions acts as a kind of ideological buffer between class conditions and the state. This is an important consideration when thinking about de Tocqueville's analysis, because his major fear for American democracy is that what he sees as equality of conditions can lead, paradoxically, to a dangerous concentration of political power—the only kind of despotism that young America had to fear.

It would probably not be too scandalous to suggest that de Tocqueville's fears had been realized to a great degree by the end of the twentieth century. And the current climate, where the "tutelary" government threatens freedom in all kinds of ways in the name of wars it says are not arguable, could only be chilling to de Tocqueville's sense of the virtues of democracy. The (re)consolidation of this kind of tutelary power is figured for me in the colossal gaze I've talked about, a gaze that construes a "you" by way of narratives of catastrophe and panic, while extending the power of its gaze across the globe by whatever means necessary.

But at the center of this dialectic of freedom and equality, almost as their motor, de Tocqueville installs the idea that American subjects are finally "confined entirely within the solitude of their own heart," that they are "apt to imagine that their whole destiny is in their own hands," and that "the practice of Americans leads their minds to fixing the standards of judgement in themselves alone" (240–41). It's true that for de Tocqueville this kind of inflection is not irredeemably bad: he sees it, after all, as a condition of freedom itself. But nonetheless, the question remains open for him: whether or not the quotidian and self-absorbed interest of the individual could ever be the operating principle for a successful nation. He is essentially asking whether the contractual and civil benefits of freedom can in the end outweigh the solipsistic and individualistic effects of a putative equality. Or, to put the issue differently, he is asking about the consequences of allowing a certain kind of narcissism to outweigh any sense of the larger historical processes of the commonwealth. This is a foundational question, if ever there was one, in the history of the nation.

Jean Baudrillard's *America,* written in part as a kind of "updating" of de Tocqueville at the end of the twentieth century, is instructive for the way it assumes that de Tocqueville's questions are still alive—or at least, it assumes that Americans themselves have changed very little in almost two hundred years (90). Baudrillard is in agreement with de Tocqueville that the interplay of freedom and equality, and their relation to democratic institutions, is what lies at the heart of America's uniqueness. He's equally clear, however, that the twentieth century has seen not the maintenance of freedom (elsewhere he is critical of the way that tutelary power has led to regulation and not freedom), but the expansion of a *cult* of equality. What has happened since de Tocqueville is the "irrepressible development of equality, banality, and indifference" (89). In the dialectic of freedom and equality, such a cult necessarily diminishes the extent of freedom, and this is clearly a current that the present U.S. regime is content to steer. But Baudrillard, like de Tocqueville, remains essentially enthralled by the "overall dynamism" in that process, despite its evident downside; it is, he says, "so exciting" (89). And he identifies the drive to equality rather than freedom as the source of the peculiar energy of America. In a sense, he might well be right: certainly it is this "dynamism" that "we" love, even as "we" might resist and resent the master's gaze upon which it battens. And yet, each celebration of the "conditions of equality" adds to the long tradition of ignoring and eliding the material conditions of inequality that in fact undergird all of America's dynamism.

## love and contradiction

This "dynamism" in American culture has been sold to "us" as much as to "you"—perhaps even more determinedly and extensively in some ways. "Brand America" has been successfully advertised all around the world, in ways and places and to an extent that most Americans are probably largely unaware of. While Americans would probably have some consciousness of the reach of the corporate media, or of Hollywood, and necessarily some idea of the reach of other brands such as McDonald's, most could not have much understanding of how the very idea of America has been sold and bought abroad. For many of "us," of course, it is the media and Hollywood that have provided the paradigmatic images and imaginaries of this dynamic America. It is, in fact, remarkable how many of the writers in the issue of *Granta* in which Doris Lessing's essay appears mention something about the way those images took hold for them, in a process of induction that "we" can be sure most Americans do not experience reciprocally.

The dynamism of that imaginary America is a multifaceted thing, imbuing the totality of social relations and cultural and political practices. It begins, maybe, with a conveyed sense of the utter modernity of American life and praxis, a modernity aided and abetted by the vast array of technological means of both production and consumption. The unstinting determination of the culture to be mobile, to be constantly in communicative circuits and to be open day and night, along with the relative ease and efficiency of everyday life and the freedom and continuousness of movement, all combine to produce a sense of a culture that is endemically alive and happening. This is "our" sense of an urban America, at least, with its endless array of choices and the promised excitement and eroticism of opportunity. The lure of that kind of urbanity was always inspissated by the "melting pot" image of the United States, and is further emphasized in these days of multiculturalism and multiethnicity. Even beyond the urban centers, of which there are so many, this dynamic life can be taken for granted, and the realm of the consumer and the obsessive cheapness of that realm reflect the concomitant sense of a nation fully endowed with resources—material and human—and with a standard of living enjoyed by most people, but achieved by very few outside the United States—even these days, and even in the other postindustrial democracies. "We" can also see this vitality of the everyday life readily reflected in the institutional structures of the United States: for instance, other ways in which we are sold America include the arts, the sciences, sports, and the educational system, and "we" derive from each of those realms the same sense of a nation on the move. As "our" Americans friends might say, what's not to like?

Beyond the realms of culture and everyday life, "we" are also sold the idea of America as a progressive and open political system, the likes of which the world has never seen before. The notions that concern de Tocqueville so much are part of this, of course: freedom, equality, and democratic institutions are the backbone of "our" political imaginary about the United States. In addition, "we" are to understand America as the home of free speech, freedom of the press and the media, and all the other crucial rights that are enshrined in the Constitution and the Bill of Rights. Most important, "we" understand those rights to be a matter for perpetual discussion, fine-tuning, and elaboration in the context of an open framework of governance, legislation, and enforcement. Even though those processes are immensely complex, "we" assume their openness and efficacy. Even the American way of doing bureaucracy seems to "us" relatively smooth, efficient, and courteous, as it does its best to emulate the customer-seeking practices of the service industries. And all this operates in the service less of freedom and more, as I've suggested, in the service of "equality of condition"—and ultimately in the service of a meritocratic way of life that even other democratic nations can't emulate. And on a more abstract level, I was struck recently by the words of the outgoing Irish ambassador to the United States, Sean O'Huiginn, who spoke of what he admired in the American character: the "real steel behind the veneer of a casual liberal society . . . the strength and dignity [and] good heartedness of the people" and the fact that America had "brought real respect to the rule of law" (*Washington Post,* July 12, 2002).

These features, and I'm sure many others, are what go to constitute the incredibly complex warp and woof of "our" imaginaries of the United States. The reality of each and any of them, and necessarily of the totality, is evidently more problematic. The words of another departing visitor, the British journalist Matthew Engel, are telling: "The religiosity, the prohibitionist instincts, the strange sense of social order you get in a country that has successfully outlawed jaywalking, the gluttony, the workaholism, the bureaucratic inflexibility, the paranoia and the national weakness for ill-informed solipsism have all seemed very foreign" (*The Guardian,* June 3, 2003). And still to be added to that list of perhaps venal sins, there is the very real horror of "your" everyday barbaric attachment to the most primitive of punishments—the death penalty. But still, those imaginaries are nonetheless part of "our" relation to America—sufficiently so that in the immediate 9/11 aftermath the question so often asked by Americans ("Why do they hate us?") seemed to me to miss the point quite badly. That is, insofar as the "they" to whom the question refers is a construct similar to the "we" that I've been talking about, "we" don't hate "you," but rather *lovehate* "you."

Nor is it a matter, as so much American public discourse solipsistically likes to insist, of "our" envying or being jealous of America. Indeed, it is another disturbing symptom of the narcissistic colossus to constantly imagine that everyone else is jealous or envious. Rather, "we" are caught in the very same contradictions the master is caught in. For every one of the features that constitutes our imaginary of dynamic America, we find its underbelly. Or rather, we find the other movement of a dialectic—the attenuation of freedom in the indifferentiation of an assumed equality, or the great barbarity at the heart of a prized civility, for instance. Equally, accompanying all of the achievements installed in this great imaginary of America, there is a negative side. For instance, while on the one hand there is the dynamic proliferation of technologies of communication and mobility, on the other hand there is the militarism that gave birth to much of the technology, and an imperious thirst for the oil and energy that drive it. And within the movement of that dialectic—one, it should be said, whose preeminence in the functioning of America has been confirmed once more since 9/11—lies the characteristic forgetting and ignorance that subvent the imaginary. That is, such technologies come to be seen only as naturalized products of an ex-historical process, and their rootedness in the processes of capital's exploitation of labor is more or less simply elided. And to go further, for all the communicative ease and freedom of movement, there is the extraordinary ecological damage caused by the conduct of everyday American life and consumption—as in the travel system, for instance. Yet this cost is also largely ignored—by government and people alike—even while the tension between capital accumulation and the ecological comes to seem more and more, as Ellen Wood (2002) has argued, the central contradiction in American capitalism today.

One could easily go on: the point is that from every part of the dynamic imaginary of America, an easy contradiction flows. Despite, for example, the supposed respect for the rule of law, American citizens experience every day what Baudrillard in *America* rightly calls "autistic and reactionary violence" (45); and the ideology of the rule of law does not prevent the United States from being opposed to the World Court, or regularly breaking treaties, or picking and choosing which United Nations resolutions need to be enforced, or illegally invading and occupying sovereign nations while menacing others. The imaginary of America, then, that "we" are sold—and which I'm sure "you" believe that "we" *should* be sold—is caught up in these kinds of contradictions—contradictions that both enable it and produce its progressive realities. These contradictions in the end constitute the very conditions of this capitalism, which is fundamentalist in its practice and ideologies.

So "our" love for America, either for its symbols and concepts or for its realities, cannot amount to some sort of corrosive jealousy or envy. It is considerably more complex and overdetermined than that. It is, to be sure, partly a coerced love, as "we" stand structurally positioned to feed the narcissism of the master. And it is in part a genuine admiration for what I'm calling for shorthand the "dynamism" of America. But it is a love and admiration shot through with ressentiment, and in that sense it is "about" American economic, political, and military power and the blind regard that those things treat "us" to. It is the coincidence of the contradictions within America's extremist capitalism, the non-seeing gaze of the master, and "our" identification with and ressentiment toward America that I'm trying to get at here. Where those things meet and interfere is the locus of "our" ambivalence toward "you," to be sure, but also the locus of "your" own confusion and ignorance about "us"—and, therefore, "your" habitual antagonism and aggression. But the "yea or nay" positivist mode of American culture will not often countenance the representation of these complexities; they just become added to the pile of things that cannot be said, especially in times of catastrophe, panic, and endless war.

# what if not allowed to be said

*i*t is easy enough to list the kinds of things that could not be said or mentioned immediately after 9/11, or to enumerate the sorts of speech that were disallowed, submerged, or simply ignored as the narratives of panic and catastrophe set in to reorder "you" and begin the by-now lengthy process of attenuating freedom. Among the things that were not allowed to be said or mentioned was President Bush's disappearance or absence the morning of the attacks. The media also very quickly elided contradictions in the incoming news reports about not only the terrorist airplanes, but about any possible defensive ones. It's still possible to be called a conspiracy theorist for wondering about the deployment of U.S. warplanes that day, as Gore Vidal discovered when he published such questions in an article provocatively titled "The Enemy Within" (*The Observer,* October 27, 2002). The idea that the attacks would never have happened if Bush had not become president was proscribed; and so on. Questions of that sort were minimally addressed, if at all, by the 9/11 Commission, whose report was a bestseller in the United States. In addition, all kinds of assaults were made on people who had dared to say something "off-message": comedians lost their jobs for saying that the terrorists were not cowards, as Bush had said they were, if they were willing to give up their lives; college presidents and reputable academics were charged with being the weak link in America's response to the attacks; and many other, varied incidents of the sort occurred, including physical attacks on Muslims simply for being Muslim. And in the years since the attacks, despite the evident weight that 9/11 exerts on public discourse, many questions and issues are still passed over in silence by the media and therefore do not come to figure in the construction of a free dialogue about "your" response to the event.

Many of "us" were simply silenced by the solipsistic "grief" (how one might like to have had that word reserved for more private and intimate relationships!) and the extreme shock of Americans around us. David Harvey, in his essay, "Cracks in the Edifice of the Empire State"

(2002), talks about how impossible it was to raise a critical voice about the role that bond traders and their ilk in the burning towers might have had in the creation and perpetuation of global social inequality (59). Noam Chomsky was rounded upon by all and sundry for suggesting, in the way of Malcolm X, that the chickens had come home to roost. The last thing that could be suggested was the idea that, to put it bluntly, these attacks were not unprovoked and anybody who thought there could be a logic to them beyond their simple evilness was subjected to the treatment that Lessing describes in my opening quotation.

The bafflement that so many of "you" expressed at the idea that someone could do this deed, and further that not all of "us" were necessarily so shocked by it, was more than just the emotional reaction of the moment. This was an entirely predictable inflection of a familiar American extremism, soon hardening into a defiant—and often reactionary— refusal to consider any response other than the ones "you" were being offered by political and civic leaders and the media. Empirical and material, political and economic realities were left aside, ignored, not even argued against, but simply considered irrelevant and even insulting to the needs of a "grief" that suddenly became national—or rather, that suddenly found a cohesive "you." And that "grief" turned quickly into a kind of sentimentality—remembering that sentimentality is famously defined by Wallace Stevens as a failure of feeling. But much more than a failure of feeling, it was a failure, in the end, of historical intelligence. A seamless belief that America can do no wrong and a hallowed and defiant ignorance about history constitute no kind of response to an essentially political event. Even when the worst kinds of tragedy strike, an inability to take any kind of responsibility or feel any kind of guilt is no more than a form of narcissistic extremism in and of itself.

## narcissistic symbols

On 9/11, there were initially some media discussions about how the Twin Towers might have been chosen for destruction because of their function as symbols of American capitalist power in the age of globalization. David Harvey suggests in his essay that in fact it was only in the non-American media that such an understanding was made available, and that the American media talked instead about the towers simply as symbols of American values and freedom, or the American way of life (57). My memory, though, is that the primary American media, in the first blush of horrified reaction, did indeed talk about the towers as symbols of economic might, and about the Pentagon as a symbol of military power. But like many other things that could not be said, or could no longer be said at that horrible time, these notions were quickly made to disappear. Strangely, the Pentagon attack soon became so unsymbolic as to be almost ignored. The Twin Towers in New York then became the center of attention, perhaps because they were easier to parlay into symbols of generalized American values than the dark Pentagon, and because the miserable deaths of all those civilians was more easily identifiable than the smaller number of military workers in Washington.

This was a remarkable instance of the way an official line can silently, almost magically, gel in the media. But more important, it is an example of the kind of ideological movement I've been trying to talk about so far: a movement of obfuscation, essentially, whereby even the simplest structural and economic realities of America's condition are displaced from discourse. As Harvey suggests, the attacks could hardly be mistaken for anything but a direct assault on the circulatory heart of financial capital: "Capital, Marx never tired of emphasizing, is a process of circulation. . . . Cut the circulation process for even a day or two, and severe damage is done. . . . What bin Laden's strike did so brilliantly was [to hit] hard at the symbolic center of the system and expose its vulnerability" (64–65).

The Twin Towers were a remarkable and egregious architectural entity, perfectly capable of bearing all kinds of allegorical reading. But there surely can be no doubt that they were a crucial "symbolic center" of the processes through which global capitalism exercises itself. Such a reading of their symbolism makes more sense than Immanuel Wallerstein's metaphorical understanding, described in his essay, "America and the World: The Twin Towers as Metaphor" (2001) that "they signalled technological achievement; they signalled a beacon to the world." And it is perhaps also more telling than (though closer to) Baudrillard's understanding of them: "Allergy to any definitive order, to any definitive power is—happily—universal, and the two towers of the World Trade Center were perfect embodiments, in their very twinness, of that definitive order" (*The Spirit of Terrorism*, 6). It is certainly an understanding that not only trumps, but exposes the very structure of the narcissistic reading of them as symbols of "your" values and "your" freedom.

That narcissism was, however, already there to be read in these Twin Towers, which stared blankly at each other, catching their own reflections in an endless relay. They were, that is, not only the vulnerable and uneasy nerve centers of the process of capital circulation and accumulation; they were also massive hubristic tributes to the self-reflecting narcissism they served. Perhaps it was something about their arrogant yet blank, unsympathetic yet entitled solipsism that suggested them as targets. The attacks implied at the very least that someone out there was fully aware of the way the narcissist's identity and the identity of those the narcissist overlooks are historically bound together. It's harder to discern whether those people would have known, too, that the narcissist is not easy to cure, however often targeted; or whether they predicted or could have predicted, and perhaps even desired, the normative retaliatory rage that their assault would provoke.

What "we" know, however, is that "we" cannot forever be the sufficient suppliers of the love that the narcissist finds so necessary. Indeed, "we" know that it is part of the narcissistic disorder to believe that "we" should be both able and obliged to be so. But so long as the disorder is rampant, "we" are, in fact, under an ethical obligation not to be such a supplier. In that sense (and contrary to all the annoying post–9/11 squealing about how "we" should not be anti-American), "we" are obliged to remind the narcissist of the need to develop what Christopher Lasch calls "the moral realism that makes it possible for [you] to come to terms with existential constraints on [your] power and freedom" (249).

But those sentiments—Lasch's final words in a retrospective look at his famous work, *The Culture of Narcissism* (1978)—are not really quite enough. To leave the matter there would be to define it as an exclusively ethical one, hoping for some kind of moral conversion—and this is not an auspicious hope where the narcissistic master is concerned. At the current moment, when we all—"we" and "you"—have seen the violent retaliation of the colossus and are confronting the reality of extraordinary violence on a world scale, too much discussion and commentary (both from the right and the left) remain at the moral or ethical levels. This catastrophic event and the perpetual war that has followed it have obviously, in that sense, produced an obfuscation of the political and economic history that surrounds them and of which they are part. Such obfuscation serves only the master and does nothing to recognize—let alone to satisfy—the legitimate ressentiment of a world laid out at the master's feet. At the very least, in the current conjuncture, "we all" need to understand that the fundamentalisms and extremisms that the master promulgates, and to which "you" are in thrall, are not simply moral or ethical, or even in any sense discretely political; they are just as much economic, and it is that aspect of them that is covered over by the narcissistic symptoms of a nation that speaks through and as "you."

## narcissistic refraction

_f_or Jean Baudrillard, during his travels around America in the 1980s, a notably recurring feature was a solitary, isolated figure in the midst of the hyperactivity of the culture, like the skateboarder with a Walkman rolling around the cityscape. Everywhere, he says, "you find the same blank solitude, the same narcissistic refraction" (34). Baudrillard's idiosyncratic travelogue, _America,_ is in many respects intended as a twentieth-century commentary on de Tocqueville and on a whole tradition of critical "Old World" views of the American republic, and seems as much a critique of the chronically patronizing and disapproving stance of the old Europeans as a description of America.

At the same time, Baudrillard's attempts to look benevolently on the extremism of American culture are ambivalent at best. The narcissistic refraction he finds everywhere is one instance of this ambivalence. That is, Baudrillard is merely a spectator, determinedly nothing more

than a voyeur in relation to the narcissistic display, and he thus avoids
or cannot confront the essential questions that de Tocqueville poses.
Can the solipsism of a "you," convinced of its rights and the principle of
equality, ever be sufficient support for the juridical concept of freedom embraced by the economic interests of the republic? Or, could the
boons of civic and economic freedom ever neutralize the rampant individualism, the narcissistic refraction, of subjects?

What is at stake in such questions is, in the end, the dialectic
between the ideal of a public realm founded in economic rights and
the ideal of a private realm founded in an ideology of individualism (a
dialectic that is reminiscent, of course, of the central contradiction in
capitalism that Marx described, between social production and private
ownership). Over the years, other commentators on America under
various rubrics and in various guises have endlessly dealt with the contradiction here. But the issue that still usually remains obscured is the
effort of the American republic to regulate not just the economic rules,
but also the very nature of the subject and its "individualism"—just as
any regime of accumulation entails the production of a regulated, regular subject. Although, in a wishful scenario, the "narcissistic refraction"
of American subjects could be understood as a kind of resistance precisely to their subjection, in the end the history of American capitalist
culture suggests an opposite kind of conclusion, one where the notions
of equality and individualism have come to be the appropriate *supports*
for the regulation of subjects. The genius of American capitalism has
been, in that sense, to elide the inherent contradiction between freedom
and equality. "Narcissistic refraction," that is to say, is another name for
regulated subjectivity.

The interplay of freedom and equality, then (to remain with de
Tocqueville's terms, and thus the terms of so many other discussions) is
a dialectic than runs through the history of American culture. But iron-
ically, the maintenance of that dialectic demands the removal or the
elision of its concrete history. As I noted before, it demands even of
de Tocqueville himself a willingness to believe in an ideological and
materially inaccurate notion of the "equality" existing in the nineteenth
century. Or today, it demands, for example, that most of "you" should
forget or not know that the founding fathers considered negroes to be

property and to be only a fraction of a person. Indeed, the Constitution itself demonstrates that individual rights are essentially an afterthought, appended in the Bill of Rights; constitutional and legal history underline the fact that individual rights must be permanently and routinely subordinated to economic interests. American subjects are, that is, interpellated under the banner of equality at the expense of an elision of their own concrete economic realities and the history of those realities. Again, there is in this situation a reminder of Marx, who points out capital's need for subjects who will think themselves free to sell their labor time to capital—even though their alternative is nonsurvival.

So, the interpellation of a "you" demands the elision of history and concrete material facts, while encouraging a narcissistic refraction that rests on a basic belief in equality. But such a narcissism is thus inevitably a contradiction, unstable and fragile, since it is deprived of a historical and concrete relation to real conditions and because it is invested instead in a notion, equality, that prima facie elides the historical and the concrete. That fragility is, of course, built in to the very structure of narcissism. Hubert Damisch, long before 9/11, surveys "the Narcissus known as Manhattan" (94), noting the way the city's gaze is turned upon its own reflection in the sky, and recalls the end of the Narcissus myth. The self-absorbed gaze "entails the risk of Narcissus dying a symbolic death, perishing through his own eyes." That is to say, the myth of Narcissus is essentially a parable about the vulnerability of the narcissist, the fragility of a subject underdeveloped in its relation to real conditions.

For psychoanalysis, of course, narcissism is properly a primitive state, primal narcissism being a moment in subject development before the primitive store of libidinal energy has been made to attach to external objects in what Freud calls an anaclitic fashion. The existence of narcissistic symptoms in noninfants is thus a disorder, characterized by emotional grandiosity and arrogance, lack of affect toward others, lack of commitment to the external world, and so on. Narcissists require recognition of their superiority, entertain fantasies of their own power or omnipotence, are convinced of their uniqueness, need special admiration, adulation, attention, and affirmation—or else they wish to be feared; they cannot react positively to criticism, they feel entitled to admiration and worthy of special treatment, and yet at the same time they are incapable of empathy for the feelings and needs of others. Their own arrogant behaviors are often accompanied by rage and violence when contradicted or thwarted. Importantly, the narcissist's self-image inevitably produces its own underbelly—a sense of low self-esteem, an uncertainty about "your" own value, "your" own ability to measure up. As Erich Fromm has pointed out in his *Escape from Freedom* (1941), while the classic Freudian view is that the narcissist "has withdrawn his love from others and turned it towards his own person," in fact "he loves neither others nor himself" (116).

It would be something of a rote exercise to detail to what extent the narcissist's list of symptoms was on display in America after 9/11, not just immediately after the attacks, but equally in the succeeding years. One remarkable feature of the immediate aftermath, however, was the sudden emergence of what Gilbert Achcar calls in his book *The Clash of Barbarisms* (2002) "narcissistic compassion." As I've suggested in my *Millennial Dreams* (1997), this is a land that has no collective history, but only personal histories and anecdotes, yet there suddenly arose an affectation of community where none had previously existed; ties and friendships and acquaintances were suddenly invented, and people grieved extravagantly for unknown others.

This response quickly dissipated and the chronic order of American memory was restored. As a stopgap in the effort to recover from the shock, the "nation" had cast its mind back to some ideal, utopian moment of American comity. That reaching back (a reflex for the narcissist in moments of crisis in the supply of narcissistic support) soon becomes unnecessary and the hard, stony attitude of narcissistic inflection returns. But, according to Achcar, the notion of "narcissistic compassion—going beyond any legitimate compassion for any human being victimized by a barbaric act—makes it possible to understand the formidable, absolutely exceptional intensity of the emotions and passions that seized hold of 'public opinion' after the attacks" (22). Achcar is speaking primarily of the fulsome reaction in other northern countries to the attacks on America, but the idea of this "narcissistic compassion" applies well to the kind of displays that the American, media-led responses produced. The shock of 9/11 and the "grief" it induced are, dare I say, factitious and somewhat ephemeral. The event threatens the more or less comfortable tension in the dialectic of freedom and equality that I have been speaking of, to be sure. But by dint of the narcissistic refraction that passes through a stage of replenishing compassion, that chronic tension can soon be restored.

It should be clear from what I've said so far that the way I have been using the idea of narcissism is not to impute a psychological disorder to individual subjects. Rather, I mean to use the term as a way of describing the broad outlines of a more generalized sociocultural structure and, here, to account for the peculiar refraction, or what we might call the subject's border in relation to the ideological "proferring" of freedom. At the same time, it's not hard to agree with Herbert Marcuse when he suggests that "the strains and stresses suffered by the individual in . . . society are grounded in the normal functioning of that society (and of the individual!) rather than in its disturbances and diseases" (249). The "normal functioning" of American society, as I've been proposing, is constituted in large part by this dialectical play between the notions of freedom and equality. Where the narcissistic colossus assumes its peculiar ichnographic stance over the world it views, there is a corresponding narcissistic refraction in the subject, in the "you" that is the desired and normative—that is, regulated—subject.

Marcuse notes that the interpellation of a "you" involves making the subject "capable of being ill, of living his sickness as health, without noticing that he is sick precisely [because] he sees himself and is seen as healthy and normal" (250). Marcuse's "diagnosis" is intended to describe the period of the so-called affluent society in post–World War II America, and particularly the time of the Vietnam War, when he writes. His sense of the social subject and the forces at play in its production and regulation derives from his analysis of the march of "advanced industrial society," along with its massive technologization and alienation. This advanced industrial society, like any other, demands that the individual be reconciled with the kind of existence and the specific conditions that the state and capital require. In that society the subject experiences what Marcuse calls "super-sublimation," such that not just the state violence of the Vietnam War, but equally the subject's everyday life and work, appear disjunct from the subject's control. In the end, Marcuse's description produces an elaborated concept of alienation, and one that has taken fuller and fuller effect in the years since he wrote. Those years have induced not only the ever deepening alienation of work and everyday life, but perhaps also the alienation of subjects from the political realm in the current moment. Certainly, one of the principal symptoms Marcuse describes is one that can be applied to the post–9/11 conjuncture, namely the weakening of "personal responsibility, conscience, and the sense of guilt" (263). The narcissist's lack of empathy is constituted by those deficits, and each of them is a function of alienation.

## *subject of value*

*H*erbert Marcuse's form of social psychology has certainly been more highly regarded than it is now. The same could be said of the work of several of his Frankfurt School colleagues that, however variously, attempted to delineate the structure of a social subject under advanced capitalism (along with Marcuse's own "one-dimensional man," one thinks of Adorno's "authoritarian personality," or Fromm's "man for himself," for instance). But despite some well-established difficulties with this kind of work, it seems clear that the effort to examine the dialectic of subject and structure (a mainstay for generations of sociologists) remains a crucial analytical task for understanding contemporary cultures, and the benefit of Marcuse's work in this regard is his determination to ground sociocultural behaviors and traits in the conditions of an advanced capitalist economy. As Erich Fromm has pointed out in "Politics and Psychoanalysis," such an aim demands an "exact knowledge of the economic, social and political situation" in which subjects find themselves (216).

If Fromm commits the fundamental error of positing a deterministic relation between those conditions and the subjects living in them, most contemporary work in cultural studies more often than not makes the mistake of denying or underplaying any such relation at all. The same criticisms can be made of the work that most overtly deploys a notion of narcissism as a description of a generalized American subject, namely, Christopher Lasch's well-known account of the whole culture, *The Culture of Narcissism*. Writing in the 1970s, Lasch sees a culture, founded on the notion of competitive individualism, that carries the logic of competition and consumerist acquisitiveness to a "dead end in a narcissistic preoccupation with the self" (xv). The symptoms he perceives of narcissistic preoccupation are similar to the designations I talked about above, though Lasch stresses the inwardness of the narcissist and the selfish acquisitiveness that answers the stress of postindustrial capitalist life. According to Lasch, that culture produces stress through alienation, and thence isolation and further alienation—this is the dead end he refers to, a point of exacerbated alienation. The same sense of fragility and vulnerability I've talked about also attends the subject's narcissism in Lasch's account.

The influence of the Frankfurt School on Lasch's work is very obvious, even if he suggests that their attempt to construe a social subject in the form of the "authoritarian personality" has been outmoded by the progress of capitalism itself (xvi), and even if he criticizes Fromm in particular for his deviations from Freud (31–32). Like the Frankfurt School writers, however, Lasch nonetheless believes that "every age develops its own peculiar forms of pathology, which express in exaggerated form its underlying character structure" (41). Such a view is evidently comparable to Fromm's idea that "every form of society has not only its own economic and political, but also its specific libidinous structures" (1989, 216). And Lasch also shares with those whom he is otherwise rejecting a central methodological assumption: namely, that the specific conditions of postindustrial capitalism more or less directly produce particular psychological symptoms in existing subjects. This deterministic view has been criticized, of course, and in the end it has to be admitted that Lasch's work ignores the very caveat that he at one point cites from Adorno, to the effect that psychoanalytical theory should remain in the realm of the individual; the temptation to homologize the structure of the subject and the conditions of society is always doomed to be overreaching.

The point here, of course, is an important methodological one. The subject in question—the "you"—is not the individual, or any individual in particular. In the same way, the forces that help construe the subject are not some coordinated set of knowing policies or deliberate actions. In this regard, Marcuse speaks helpfully of "tendencies": forces that can be identified "by an analysis of the existing society and which assert themselves even if [people] are not aware of them." Those tendencies, of course, do derive from the needs of the state and capital and serve "the requirements of the established apparatus of production, distribution and consumption." They are constituted in the "economic, technical, political, mental requirements which have to be fulfilled in order to assure the continued functioning of the apparatus on which the population depends, and the continuing function of the social relationships derived from the organization of the apparatus" (252). These "tendencies" are, in sum, the "proferred" ideological script for the subject, and they may or may not be fulfilled. I mean that neologism (taken from my book, *Discerning the Subject* [1988]), as a play on the words "prefer" and "proffer"—these are, then, the preferred offerings for the subject to take up. But they do respond to the fact that under capitalism, as Marcuse says, "social needs must become individual needs" (253), and they thus serve as attempts to regulate the subject, even if they cannot guarantee their own success.

This is a view of the workings of ideology that Lasch certainly does not inherit from the Frankfurt School, and his own more deterministic view remains a great flaw in his work. But the central criticism that needs to be made of *The Culture of Narcissism* is of a different order and concerns another methodological question, already alluded to. That is, although Lasch is at pains to suggest that the narcissist he sees in U.S. culture is the "final product of bourgeois individualism" and the product of a particular stage of U.S. capitalism—the beginning of the postindustrial moment—his work takes much of the description of that moment for granted. In other words, in Lasch's deterministic view of the subject, there is little room for sustained analysis of precisely the economic conditions and changes in which the subject is embroiled. In this sense, Lasch unfortunately prefigures much current work in cultural studies, which tends to concentrate on the epiphenomenal features of culture and subjectivity while perhaps invoking "capitalism" as an afterthought. Here again a caveat from the Frankfurt School is ignored: that any understanding of culture and subjectivity requires "exact knowledge of the economic, social and political situation." It is this exact knowledge that Lasch cannot supply, so his description of the subjects produced by it could only ever be a partial sighting at best.

The untidy process (of the sort that can be seen in any stage of capitalism) of delineating the requisite subject for the particular regime of value production and capital accumulation cannot, in any case, guarantee an outcome or a result. The conditions of subject production are as overdetermined as the overdetermination of the subject itself. What we can say, however, is that the "proferred" view of the subject in late capitalism devolves upon the alienation of the subject. Here Lasch would not, one presumes, generally disagree, but the description of particular regimes of subjectivity and the description of the conditions under which the subject lives cannot be disjunct. The alienation of the subject is not simply a cultural, behavioral, or psychological alienation, but alienation consonant with the structural conditions of the subject's life and labor. That is, the particular organization of the capital-wage relation in any given conjuncture, and its fundamental role in the structuring of the social, is ultimately the source of alienation. Thus, cultural, behavioral, or psychological practices cannot be understood without reference to the material conditions induced and caused by the wage relation.

The subject is, then, a necessarily historical entity, construed as the requisite subject for specifiable regimes and modes of value production. As I have suggested before in my *Millennial Dreams* (82–83), three particular features, each of which serves the maintenance of the existing apparatus of production and consumption including the wage relation, characterize the subject appropriate to the regimes of capital accumulation in the contemporary moment. This is what I call "the subject of value" and it is (1) endowed with an ultimately self-interested rationality, (2) convinced of the principle of equality, and (3) dedicated to the concept of private property. In the American context, the role and the power of the three designations is perhaps underscored by remembering that they are promulgated there under the rubric of "freedom."

The first crucial characteristic of this subject is the imputation of a self-interested rationality. This characteristic, a foundational assumption in neoliberal and positivist economic theory, implies a subject that is simultaneously appetitive and calculating, a subject that is, at one and the same time, able to recognize its fundamental needs and also capable of calculating the best way to attain those needs. The subject of value, then, melds what might be called a primitive or primal nature with sophisticated or developed capacities to satisfy that nature. It's interesting to note that this mix of the natural and the sophisticated by no means vitiates an instinctual appetitive nature (which neoliberal theory imputes to all human subjects). Rather, needs and desires are posited as the root or cause of rationality and of rational action, the developed faculties that then sustain the appetitive urge. This subject's primitive characteristics are thus literally rationalized, even though the constitution of either the subject's supposed needs or its putative rationality (that is, the conditions under which needs and·rationality are produced, interact, and made available to subjects) need not be questioned.

The point of this rationalization is to guarantee a subject that is warranted to be selfish and, consequently, competitive. And in its dealings with the world and with others, this subject will take those qualities to be normal, conventional, and acceptable. (To quote Marcuse's formulation again, this is a subject "capable of being ill, of living his sickness as health, without noticing that he is sick precisely [because] he sees himself and is seen as healthy and normal.") The subject's second principal characteristic—a belief in the concept of equality—has the effect of mollifying the upshot of the first. That is, the sophisticated calculation of the satisfaction of fundamental needs and desires opens the subject to a world of competing self-interests, to a game, that inevitably has winners and losers. So the principle of equality is in a sense a rule of that game, ensuring that all players, all subjects, see themselves to be at no inherent disadvantage in relation to everyone else. Equality, in other words, is a primal condition of the game, even though it disappears as the game proceeds. Nonetheless, equality is a tenet that legitimizes the competition in the first place, and subjects therefore need to be committed to its efficacy. As I've already suggested, the notion of equality is made more complex by its association with the idea of freedom: the two ideas or ideals work in tandem to legitimize each other.

The third characteristic of the subject of value is the one that most crucially ties the subject to the system of capitalism: the acceptance of the principle and the fact of private property, which for Marx is equivalent to accepting the alienation of one's own labor. Marx stresses that private property is both the goal and the consequence of the processes of primitive accumulation and capital's appropriation of labor, but it is also a necessary precondition for the continued consumption of labor power. That is, the laborer must see his or her labor time as private property that can be freely sold on the market; the laborer must be "free" exactly in order to sell labor time—even when there is no alternative. Insofar as private property is thus central to the capital-wage relation, it necessarily comes to reside at the basis of all legal and ideological enforcement. So it is property rights (rather than, say, human rights, or rights to subsistence, or rights to economic security and justice) that constitute the basis of the legal frameworks of the northern democracies. The law protects the accumulation of capital in private hands and fixes subjects in juridical relations to one another, defining their obedience to the law as a function of the existence of private property. The subject of value, that is to say, is legislated for.

Marx was clear about the relationship between private property and the law. In *The German Ideology,* he and Engels showed how modern civil law developed in symbiosis with the concept of private property, arising out of and dependent on the destruction of communitarian relationships and establishing instead juridical relations between alienated subjects through the mediation of objects (commodities). Marx is equally clear that private property stands as the very figure of alienation: private property is "on the one hand the product of alienated labor, and on the other it is the means by which labor is alienated, the realization of this alienation" (*Collected Works* 3: 279). Something nonetheless can be added to Marx's perception of the nexus of alienation, private property, and the law. That is to say, the subject of value, understanding equality and freedom as more or less synonymous, must be able to forget the history that gives rise to alienation and must be able to elide the empirical evidence of inequality. The subject of value thus cleaves to factitious rights of equality in spite of the empirical effects of capital's freedom. The subject of value is ex-historical in that sense.

# *historical fictions*

*H*ubert Damisch, in *Skyline: The Narcissistic City* (2001), says that the goal of his book's discussion of a whole range of American cultural phenomena is to locate "the moment America constituted itself, in its own eyes, as a scene on which it dreaded having to recognize itself for what it was" (88). Evidently for Damisch this is not so much a strictly historical question as a question about the American imaginary, or about America's fictions about itself. America is for him essentially "the site of its own fiction . . . the site where people turn from their past towards a future at odds with permanence" (71). Along with Damisch, one might want to suggest that these fictions may have outlasted their usefulness; their primal role in the cultural imaginary of this nation is losing its power, such that the nation might well have to, so to speak, face reality and reconstrue itself on the basis of historical and material facts. And, writing before 9/11, Damisch asks, in a strange foreboding, "but for how much longer" can these fictions remain effective?

I might be accused of misusing or misapplying Damisch's arguments here insofar as it's clear that his analysis of the founding fictions of America intends to attribute them to some European imaginary. He is, in other words, writing in the tradition of the European observer of America, part of whose concern is that America appears as a projection of European fantasies, or that it has exemplary lessons to teach "old Europe." De Tocqueville might be seen as the best example of such writers, while Baudrillard continues the tradition in a dissenting kind of way. In the end, however, this tradition has often come across the fact that the very imaginary of America becomes its history. Writers like Damisch have been able to see that the imaginary turn from the past toward an equally imaginary future at odds with permanence does in fact correspond to a material process of American culture. That is, the erasure of material history in the alienated subject and the establishment of primitive faith in myths of origin, destiny, and ideal principles are two sides of the same processs—the process that ensures the construction of the proper subject for America's extreme capitalism.

The attacks of 9/11 should, perhaps, have constituted a moment when the ex-historical obstinacy of this culture collapsed, when the founding fictions of the republic might have been shown to have outstripped their own rationale, and when the building of a new kind of historical realism and a progressive kind of social hope might have begun. That 9/11 did not finally serve as such an opportunity is, however regrettable, in fact unsurprising. The primal role of the kinds of imaginaries that Damisch analyzes is what makes them stand in for the historical real, and they are bound up in the very fabric of the operation of American society. Those historical fictions (such as the fiction of the nation's founding, of its founding fathers, of its "manifest destiny," the fiction of the frontier, and so on) bind the subject to the nation in a kind of primal symbiosis.

The origins of these fictions and their continuing strength have, of course, been the object of continued analysis and speculation in the historiography of America, as well as in many other fields, and to take account of even a portion of the scholarship on offer would be the task of another book. For my purposes here, the most helpful accounts are those proposing that the development of what might best be called American mythography is centrally related to the processes of capitalist development in America. There are, indeed, far fewer such accounts than there are analyses of the sociocultural *significations* of America's primal mythographies; and many accounts that do specify a more political-economic relation are marginalized or readily forgotten. This is perhaps predictable since, as I've been suggesting, part of the effort and effect of the American organization of the apparatus of production and consumption has been the elision of material and historical consciousness.

One "forgotten" text of this sort is *America* by the eminent Dutch historian Johan Huizinga, written in two volumes in 1918 and 1926. Huizinga addresses the foundational moments of America by drawing out a contrast with capitalist development and the production of individualism in Europe. What Huizinga calls the "primitive" or precapitalist moment in Europe had given way to the era of individualism, ushered in by the French Revolution, and the "universal" declaration of equality. Marx had seen this declaration of equality as nothing more than the establishment of the bourgeois principle "that every man is equally regarded as a self-sufficient monad" (*Collected Works* 3: 163), but Huizinga is more sanguine about it, seeing it as part of the development of Europe "on its way to a 'higher form of collectivism.'" (He might not have expected, of course, that this higher form, in the shape of the European Union, would still not be securely and effectively in place even in the twenty-first century!)

But Huizinga's point is to show that the creation of the American republic takes place without this "primitive" prehistory. Lacking an organic or native historical relation to feudalism or to the primitive social formations that evolved in Europe, the primal stage in American development is in the establishment of individualism itself. So it is America's version of individualism, then, that becomes its "primitive" moment for Huizinga: "[T]he individualism which was at work in the establishment of the American colonies reveals itself as much more of a primitive, limiting, and negative force" (16–17) than in Europe.

Huizinga's claim is that "freedom" in the American context was a notion that had, in a sense, not been historically or organically derived or evolved. Indeed, he suggests that for America, freedom is an anachronistic term in that it means the same as it did for medieval Europe: "freedom from interference" (17). More specifically, it is understood as the freedom to conduct commerce without interference, rather than as some more idealistic notion of human freedom or human dignity or human rights (as I've suggested, the latter are afterthoughts in the creation of America, arriving with the enshrinement of equality). For Huizinga, then, America's "primitive" is a kind of historical structural absence that has been factitiously covered over by a belated or anachronistic formation of individualism—the name that Huizinga gives to the freedom of commerce, rather than to the freedom of the individual (i.e., equality). In this light, it becomes clear why Huizinga feels warranted to suggest that "every political or cultural question in Americas is an economic one" (9). His fundamental effort is to show that phenomena that have been given the cloaking of political or cultural discourse depend absolutely on America's peculiar economic history, where there has been no organic relation to previous modes of production. (And in the case where there was such an organic relation—namely, to Native Americans—it was extirpated by force and violence.)

Huizinga's attempt to disclose the economic nature of "freedom" is reinforced in the second volume of *America* by what I take to be the influence of another almost forgotten figure, the historian Charles Beard and his seminal book, *An Economic Interpretation of the Constitution,* written in 1913. Beard might best be characterized, as William Appleman Williams indeed described him, as a "Tory-radical," a political conservative who nonetheless produced a radical and at the time disturbing view of American history by mapping out the role of economic interests in the framing of the U.S. Constitution. Beard suggests that it was the emergent bourgeoisie of the burgeoning republic (specifically, the holders of potential capital, bankers, manufacturers, and mercantilists) who framed the Constitution to the benefit of their own economic interests and to the detriment of agricultural interests in particular, and the interests of ordinary citizens in general. Beard stresses the fact that "the constitution was essentially an economic document based upon the concept that the fundamental private rights of property are anterior to government and morally beyond the reach of popular majorities" (324). He also demonstrates that the ratification of the Constitution was itself hardly democratic: "[A] large propertyless mass was, under the prevailing suffrage qualifications, excluded from the outset," and in the end "probably not more than one sixth of the adult males" in America actually voted for ratification (324).

What Beard's reading does not do is theorize fully the way that the economic formations at play in the constitutional conventions would develop. But clearly, the kinds of monetary holdings and property that the Constitution was framed to protect were to become the core of American industrial and expansionist capital in the nineteenth century. Beard also was unconcerned about the origin of those properties. But the economic history of the final years of the American colonies constitutes, in essence, a period of primitive accumulation where land and property are expropriated, mercantile capital is set into play, money imported from Europe begins to act as capital, and so on. And the period, like any other period of primitive accumulation, needs, in Marx's words, to be "written in the annals of humanity in characters of fire and blood" ("On the Jewish Question," 163). Williams points out that Beard—perhaps fittingly for one whose own political leanings were fundamentally conservative—was content "to confront his readers with the hard fact that it was specific Americans who made American history, and that for the most part they had acted on the basis of a materialistic calculus" (1992, 111). Beard's aim ultimately was to simply show that the specific ideas enshrined in the Constitution had to be understood as having been produced by that calculus.

Both Huizinga and Beard provide evidence for the argument that the most cherished shibboleths of American society—freedom and equality—do indeed exist in the kind of tension that I have been trying to describe, and that they function as disguises or displacements, so to speak, for the economic relations that lie behind them. The constitutional establishment of freedom for this "commercial people" simultaneously ensures the establishment of inequality, and the genius of the Constitution is to name that inequality equality. Huizinga recognizes then—even if he would perhaps not quite articulate it this way—that the genesis of the founding mythologies of America can be located in the very elision of economic realities and interests. For him, these mythographic ideas install a primitive formation at the heart of American political-economic history, even while that history presents itself as progressive.

Both of these historians see the subsequent history of America as the playing out of a dialectical tension between the interests of a concerted "commercial people" and those of a populace of legally "self-sufficient monads" (Marx). For a later historian, William Appleman Williams, the same tension is described differently: between, on the one hand, the interests of a capitalist "empire," and on the other, the interests of a community of citizens. But for Williams, as much as for earlier historians, the dialectic seems eventually to entail the denigration of the populace who, in Marcuse's terms, "must continue the struggle for existence in painful, costly, and obsolete forms" (256). Meanwhile, as Marx observed in *The Poverty of Philosophy*, freedom "is not the freedom of one individual in relation to another, but the freedom of capital" (207).

# primitive

o buttress his claim that America is "the only remaining primitive society," Jean Baudrillard rehearses the old cliché that America has no history. It is a society, he says, "inhabited by a total metasocial fact . . . whose immanence is breathtaking, yet lacking a past through which to reflect on this [it is] therefore fundamentally primitive" (*America,* 7). Baudrillard's hyperbole is, presumably, intended to equal the hyperbolic culture he sees in his American travels, but it nonetheless remains strange to talk of America as having no past, no history. Its history is, in fact, the history of elided histories, as I've been suggesting. But, of course, the net result is still the same: history cannot be used to reflect on the present and the future that is, in Damisch's words, "a future at odds with the very idea of permanence" (71). If this is a measure of primitivism, then America might indeed be said to be the only remaining primitive society.

It's not altogether clear where Baudrillard derives his notion of the primitive. While it's true that many of his rhapsodic passages on American culture appear to echo Lévi-Strauss's noted distinction between hot and cold societies, his thinking doesn't seem especially or systematically informed by anthropological discourse. Certainly, I know of no anthropological theory that elevates the process of the elision or absence of history to a centrally defining feature of primitive society. In any case, his use of the term isn't likely to endear him much to contemporary anthropologists. Although it can be argued that the term *primitive* is the one around which the whole discipline of anthropology evolved and still somewhat revolves, by and large anthropology has been trying to extirpate it from its vocabulary for half a century now.

Lévi-Strauss himself can be credited with leading the way in this regard. In addition to challenging assumptions of the superiority of the observing culture, he directly challenges the narrative of development that is (barely) hidden in the idea of the primitive. As Johannes Fabian argues, the term "*primitive,* being essentially a temporal concept, is a category, not an object, of Western thought" (18). As such, it could basically be called a purely ideological term, and one that has consistently cloaked anthropology's allochronic relation to other cultures (that is, anthropology locates the other peoples that it studies in a time other than that of the observer). Looking back over the history of anthropology, it's hard not to agree with Fabian that its relation to the other is in this regard entirely "a scandal" (143), and not least (as Fabian himself and many others have argued) for the way that the allochronic relationship has been used to produce and justify any number of imperialistic and dominatory practices, policies and, indeed, discourses. Anthropology's effort to get rid of the term *primitive* has therefore been intended to disown the imperial in some basic way.

Fabian's particular contribution to this process suggests that to conceive of the anthropological other in an isochronic, or what he calls coeval, fashion would be to redirect anthropology altogether—and notably away from its connivance with imperialist processes. The task that such a recommendation entails is that of turning what Fabian has called a concept into what he calls an object. One way that might be done would be to demonstrate that the concrete features and phenomena that have constituted the "primitive" are in fact empirically evident in "nonprimitive" cultures, such that the issue of allochronicity is bypassed. I know of no anthropological work that has explicitly set out to do this on the practical level, even if there have been many hints that it could be done. In the 1960s, when the connection between anthropological discourse and northern imperialism was more or less taken as read, some anthropologists pointed to ways in which "civilized" northern cultures resembled "the primitive." For instance, Ashley Montagu talks of how the "narrow range of emphases among modern cultures . . . could well be regarded as a sort of simplicity" akin to that of primitive cultures; Montagu also begins to think about the operation of nonrational or prerational elements inside the supposed rational structures of northern cultures (20–22). More recently Micaela Di Leonardo has produced a massive account of the interplay between anthropological concepts and the construction of U.S. culture in her *Exotics at Home* (1998) (a book that, among its other virtues, insists on the necessity of attending to the way that political economy and culture are bound together). And there are many others, including ethnographic studies of U.S. culture.

It is perhaps the work of Lucien Lévy-Bruhl that is most closely associated with delineating the primitive as a category. As much as that work has been critiqued and even demolished by anthropologists, it somehow remains strangely relevant in the sense that anthropology seems not quite able to escape the terms of Lévy-Bruhl's definitions: his sense that "primitive" cultures are prelogical or prerational, for instance; or his insistence that they cannot individuate or see difference beyond their own specific sociocultural environment; or his view that they cannot recognize or are unaffected by contradiction (for example, between the mystical and the empirical). Any of these conceptions of the "primitive" still appears, overtly or covertly, in this discipline that has tried to expunge the idea of the primitive. And certainly, as Di Leonardo shows at length, it is with the aiding and abetting of anthropology that such ideas about the anthropological other have passed into the realm of common sense in northern cultures.

Lévy-Bruhl's definitions have subsequently given rise to many debates and to many corrections and additions about what the primitive consists in, but most, if not all, of anthropology's working definitions clearly owe something to his formulations. The primitive can be defined as essentially a closed culture that rejects, ignores, or cannot recognize its outside, and such cultures foster a rigidly ethnocentric view of the world and a general indifference and lack of empathy in regard to the claims of other subjects and other cultures. From a single page of one account of anthropologists' definitions of the term, it seems that primitive culture is incurious, determinedly traditional, given over to mystical and nonrational and uncritical thinking, and deploys confused symbolisms; whereas its subjects are given over to emotion and rote habit, while being limited in their moral standards and incapable of discursive reasoning. At the same time, Montagu suggests that primitive society tends to be seen as democratically organized and generally nonhierarchical (17). Some versions of the primitive in anthropological discourse, such as George Homans's (68), will stress other factors—such as certain forms of kinship organization and degrees of literacy—but the above characteristics tend to get combined, repeated, and, essentially, presumed.

In his effort to transmute the kinds of judgments and stances that the imputation of these characteristics entails, Lévi-Strauss chose instead to speak of cold and hot social forms: static or crystallized social forms (the cold, such as kinship arrangements, food practices, and so forth), which can be differentiated from more mobile, mutating social forms (the hot, which are characterized by their acquisitiveness, inventiveness, and so on). But in the end this move is not enough to turn the concept of the primitive into an object—and not enough, to be sure, to counter Fabian's objections about anthropology's consistent habit of circumventing the coeval. Indeed, Fabian generally sees Lévi-Strauss's work (even his eventual use of neural structures) as an extension of anthropology's way of merely circumventing the demands of coevality, maintaining the distance of the observer from the observed, and consequently upholding the interests of northern domination (52–69).

A somewhat unlikely source (given the political ramifications of anthropology's discourses) for a way out of what we can call the conundrum of the primitive is in the words of the somewhat conservative functionalist anthropologist E. E. Evans-Pritchard. In considering the idea of the primitive, and particularly Lévy-Bruhl's contribution, Evans-Pritchard suggests an approach that would seem to be much more congenial to Fabian's demand for coevality. "It is not so much a question," he says, "of primitive versus civilized mentality, as the relation of two types of thought to each other in any society" (91). For my own purposes here—that is, within my own nonanthropological discourse and with my eye on America rather than some nonnorthern culture—this formula seems a promising way to imagine the kind of approach that would be necessary to designate the strange "coevality" of cultures in America. That is, the coexistence of the most progressive (and aggressive) technologized capitalism with the most "cold" forms of cultural phenomena seems to me the issue that any analysis of contemporary America needs to take into account before much can be said in the way of generalization.

The history of America clearly features a continuing and troubled dialectical play between hot and cold societal and cultural forms, so to speak; or it displays, in the same times and places, a heady mixture of the primitive and the progressive. This is to suggest, I hope, something a little different from the metropolitan/rural doublet so congenial to American mythographers; different, too, from the kind of red

state/blue state split that journalists lazily constructed in the 2004 elections. And it is something that surpasses the juxtaposition, frequently
remarked by scholars and journalists alike, between secular culture
and "faith-based" culture in the republic (though that juxtaposition
would, of course, be sufficiently appropriate fodder for an anthropology that wished to turn its attention to modern U.S. ethnoscapes and
to an assessment of America's peculiar admixture of the primitive and
the civilized).

In part, what I want to suggest is that this mixture of primitive
and civilized is a constitutive contradiction for the history of American society and culture, and that it can be derived from the kinds of
contradictions and formations that I have been discussing thus far in
this book. That is, what is for me the central contradiction of American culture, between freedom and equality, throws up the potential of
a juxtaposition of cultures: on the one hand, a "hot," even unbridled
progressivism under the banner of capital and commerce; and on the
other hand, a "cold," static and mystified traditionalism, often accompanied by fundamentalist religious beliefs and a complete capitula-
tion to the mythographies of America's founding. This "primitive"
aspect to American social formations is, as I have suggested before,
a kind of narcissistic refraction from the empirical realities and historical concreteness of the normatively (and normally) dominant processes of commerce, capital, and the state. The relationship between
this primitiveness and the forces of commerce and capital is latent, as
Huizinga argues, in the pro-morphic history of the republic. America's
premodernity, in other words, is coeval with the realization of the modern, and the nation's history is forever marked by the contradictions of
that scenario.

But I want to go further and also argue that this dialectical interplay,
crucial as it is to the constitution and consistency of America, should
in fact be seen as merely epiphenomenal. That is, the particular dialectic of hot and cold that can be seen at play in American culture and
in the history of the society is in the end driven by a larger and more
abiding static (cold) principle. *The essentially primitive aspect of America
resides in the fact that all social and cultural phenomena are dedicated to one
central process, the process of capital accumulation.* The particular features of

that process do, of course, change and progress, particularly by way of changes in the organization of the wage relation; but the fundamental principles consistently pertain in regular form. This singular dedication perhaps responds to what Baudrillard has referred to as the "total metasocial fact" that inhabits the society. The fundamental primitiveness of the society—its total dedication to the closed system by which its means of consumption and production are kept up—then fosters the tension of static and progressive forms in the life of the culture, but nonetheless remains the tutelary god of America's beginnings and its present.

# fetishism

When Marx set out to characterize the nature of the new capitalist formations around him, he frequently had recourse to a vocabulary of primitivism and mysticism, and the (well-known though often abused) concept of commodity fetishism is one of the principal examples. Commodity fetishism names the way that capitalism installs the commodity as a stand-in for direct social relations between subjects. That is, it is the name Marx gives to the specific mode of ordering human interaction in the capitalist mode of production, where objects both mediate and dictate the nature of social relations. The fetishism Marx speaks of describes more specifically the fact that "the social character of labor appears to us to be an objective character of the products themselves" (*Capital* 1: 43) and thus guarantees the appearance that value is produced by the mechanisms of the market, rather than through the activity of labor. Thus the fetish also specifically hides the central characteristic of production that makes capitalism function— that is, the exploitation of labor. The commodity itself becomes the very figure of the mystification of value. So Marx uses the concept of commodity fetishism to represent alienated social relations, the relations among subjects reduced to and hidden by the abstract form of the commodity.

Marx's use of the term *fetish* is interesting. As Anne McClintock has pointed out, in Marx's time the term was a byword for the primitive, ever since the eighteenth century, when "the French philosophe, Charles de Brosses, coined the term *fetishisme* as the term for 'primitive religion'" (181). Marx wants, then, to stress the primitive character of commodity relations and their propinquity to mystified religious thinking. He speaks of the "social hieroglyphic" that the commodity constitutes as something that arises from "the mist-enveloped regions of the religious world," and he thence critiques the "magic and necromancy" that surround it (*Capital* 1: 43–47). The point is to suggest that capitalism's social relations are perhaps just as mystified as those of previous modes of production (which were, at least in Marx's view, relatively "simple and transparent"). The primary upshot of this mystification is that the "determination of the magnitude of value is therefore a secret, hidden under the apparent fluctuations in the relative values of commodities" (*Capital* 1: 46).

According to McClintock, Marx, like his contemporaries, deploys the figure of the fetish as a way of ordering the uncontrollable or the incomprehensible around what she calls the "invented domain of the primitive" (182). Such a gesture, she suggests, in its reliance on the factitious or imaginary idea of the primitive, replicates and ensures the presence of the West's racism and imperialism in the heart of its conceptual frameworks — she tracks this in Freud as well, for instance. But McClintock's emphasis runs the risk of downplaying the critical element of Marx's description. The power of the concept of commodity fetishism is that it captures the quasi-mystical motor at the heart of the capitalist process. That is, the complete description of capitalism has to be able to grasp both the establishment of a process (the system of the exchange of commodities) and capitalism's way of hiding the reality of that process (making the commodity stand in for actual relations). Instead, then, of rushing to implicate Marx in the worst aspects of modernity's heritage and thereby fault his contribution, it is perhaps better to try to recognize the rhetorical force of his description. When Marx points to capital's commodity fetishism or points up the aura of religiosity and necromancy surrounding capitalist formations, what emerges is the image of a contradiction — an image, that is, of *the primitive in the heart of the supposedly modern*. It is Marx's case that the functioning of capital depends on this simultaneity of the "hot" and the "cold," to pick up Lévi-Strauss's terms once more, in its processes.

Despite capital's claims to enlightenment and progressive social effect, then, the reality of its processes suggests that this new mode of production has not thrown off the mystificatory thinking of pre-Enlightenment times. Indeed, capital precisely deploys a kind of atavistic mystification to hide the brutal realities of its rule. Not only does capital deploy such "magic and necromancy," it also marshals the service of religiosity. Marx suggests that Christianity (he does not specify what brand) is the most fitting form of religion for capital because of what he calls its "*cultus* of abstract man" (*Capital* 1: 51). Christianity prepares a subject that is suited to the alienated status of the human under capital.

So this use of the vocabulary of the primitive fetish in Marx is intended to describe the symbiotic relationship between the progressive and the modern nature of capital itself and the mystified and archaic nature of the ideological formations that are its supports. It is also intended to show a subject alienated not just at the level of material relations, but at the level of consciousness and belief. That subject, given over to commodity fetishism, is susceptible to ever-deepening alienation, as more and more of the world is commodified under capital's control (or as capital continually expands the means of consumption). The narcissistic refraction that I have talked about before is perhaps an inevitable sign of the subject under capital, registering a kind of numbness and wonderment at a world in which all social relations are best represented by commodities in the chain of commodities, and where the commodity does the work of desiring, of understanding, and of producing meaning.

# *atavism*

*t*he world that the regime of commodity fetishism generates, now indisputably a global effort in the expansion of the means of consumption, is experienced differentially by different nations, groups, classes. I borrow the expression "experienced differentially" from Kevin Robins, whose 1997 account of the cultural processes of globalization, "What in the World's Going On?" rightly emphasizes the ways that access to the culture is unevenly distributed. That is to say, while the seductions of consumerism are audible to more and more people's ears around the globe, access to the commodities themselves is less and less equal. The Retort group, in its impressive post–9/11 disquisition, *Afflicted Powers: Capital and Spectacle in a New Age of War* (2005), points out that the world is now in an "unprecedented situation" as a result of the effort to fully globalize the regime of consumption:

> [N]ever before—this is the truly chilling reality—have
> the wretched of the earth existed in such a bewildering
> and enraging hybrid state, with the imagery of consumer
> contentment piped directly into slum dormitories rented
> out by the night at cutthroat prices to hopelessly indebted
> neo-serfs. (173)

Retort's rhetoric is perhaps a little lurid, but the underlying accuracy of the image cannot be doubted—though it's necessary to stipulate that these subjects, the wretched of the earth in their slum dormitories, are to be found everywhere. It's not just in Third World slums, of course, but equally in the cities and heartlands of America itself that the globalizing regime of commodity fetishism produces startlingly unequal conditions. The aftermath of Hurricane Katrina dramatically opened a window onto the desperation of everyday conditions in one of the most famous cities in America. For a few weeks, the American media allowed a glimpse of the massive contradiction built in, as it were, to this city: between New Orleans as the quintessential city-as-commodity on the one hand, and the desperation of the lives of the "serfs" (or maybe better, the slaves) living there on the other.

The Retort group understands and explicates clearly the fundamental nature and power of commodity fetishism and the appeal of its seductions for the consumer in the moneyed enclaves of the North. By the same token, it also necessarily comprehends the resistance and hostility to the cultures of consumption that globalization produces. People whose labor has been hidden in the fetish of the commodity and those who have yet to be fully drawn into the fully functioning wage relation of capital are subjects who have not been or cannot be socialized into the new consumptive regime, and for them the attractions of the commodity regime are unattainable. In other words, the inequality that can be said to be a fundamental condition of capitalism produces its own resistance.

Retort suggests that the appeal of al-Qaida and its calls for the destruction of the North can be understood at least in part through a relationship to the world of commodity fetishism. "Among its various apprenticeships to modernity," the group says, "revolutionary Islam *has been obliged to suffer the full force of consumerism*" (180). The attacks of 9/11, as I pointed out before, can be understood as attacks on the symbolic heart of capital's global expansion, and thus as antiglobalization protests. Indeed, in his provocative account of the jihad, Faisal Devji argues that al-Qaida itself has become a global movement as a response to capital's global system, one that has removed the possibility of what he calls the politics of intentionality and autonomy: "[T]he jihad is grounded . . . in the contingent relations of a global marketplace," and shares more with movements such as environmentalism and antiglobalization organizations than it does with "the old-fashioned politics of collective unity" or national liberation movements (11).

Al-Qaida's rallying cry in its jihad against the North and globalization is a persistent reminder to its audiences of the need to undo the alienating effects of capitalist culture and life and to revivify the material social relations that capital obscures and suppresses. As Retort again points out, this is essentially a jihad against the modernity of the North. Given that the target is, exactly, modernity—the name given to the progressiveness of capital—it's hardly surprising that the proposed antidote is ancient, so to speak. Revolutionary Islam's goal of revivifying and restructuring social relations is atavistic in the sense that it proceeds under the banner of theocratic thought—and its authoritarian and masculinist ideologies follow. Even allowing for some of the complexities and complications introduced by Devji's account of the jihad (for Devji, the ultimate aim of al-Qaida is a kind of modernizing project intending "to translate Islam into the language of the ideologi-cal state" [164]), it can still be argued that an atavistic urge accompanies any modernizing tendency. It might be going overboard to talk about "Islamo-fascists" (a term coined, so far as I can tell, by that apostate from the left, Christopher Hitchens, and eagerly adopted by his new friends on the right to be applied willy-nilly to terrorists, Ba'athists, Iranians, or whomever), but there is certainly no mistaking the atavis-tic underpinnings.

Such atavistic tendencies are not the exclusive domain of revolu-tionary Islam, of course. In the United States, a similar antagonism to the alienated regime of the commodity and a similar call for the revivifica-tion of social relations are a familiar part of the cultural landscape and constitute an analogous complaint about the effects of Northern moder-nity. The case could be made that those analogous ideologies, flowing especially from the mouths of fundamentalist Christians, also serve an analogous purpose: it could be argued, that is, that fundamentalism in the United States speaks to an audience that feels itself marginalized by modernity's regime of the commodity. In the United States, how-ever, those ideologies are more often than not promulgated specifically as part of a right-wing political agenda. That is to say, the peculiar anti-modernity atavism found in the United States is more exactly an *em-powered* or *encratic* discourse, rather than the cry of the dispossessed.

One influential source of this atavism is, unsurprisingly, the cadre of neoconservatives who have inhabited George W. Bush's two adminis-trations. These are the people whom Anne Norton calls collectively the Straussians—a large group of appointees (and fellow travelers) whose commonalities include the influence of the political theorist Leo Strauss and his acolytes. Norton gives a rather uneven account of these people, including Paul Wolfowitz, William Kristol, Leon Kass, Carnes Lord, and their ilk, and I will talk about them again later in this book. Her account is vitiated somewhat by a sporadic and unsuccessful attempt to save Strauss himself from his heirs and disciples. But be that as it may, she does make clear the extent to which their ideas and prescrip-tions (now not merely prescriptions, of course, but in many instances actual policy under Bush) revolve around a disdain for the alienated re-lations of contemporary American life.

This disdain includes a rejection of the complacency and decadence considered to be induced by the regime of commodity fetishism and by the products of the culture industries in particular. But it is not only popular culture that is a symptom of deadened social relations. Carnes Lord, in his alarming treatise, *The Modern Prince* (2003), takes it upon himself to suggest remedies for the "continuing decay of moral and professional standards, civic behavior, and political engagement so evident throughout most advanced democracies today" (228). Indeed, Lord's book could serve as a guide to many of the positions of these Straussians because it presents the case for the main plank of the needed remedy: a renewed civic leadership of a kind that would recognize that power dictates freedom, and that therefore power should authorize itself to act unilaterally and in an authoritarian way to "safeguard" freedom. Lord looks forward to the establishment of the "political religion of constitutionalism that Lincoln thought essential" (230) (Lincoln is one of the principal idols of this Straussian atavism, along with Winston Churchill); and he calls for the revival of the virtues of manliness and the martial traditions. In many ways, his recommendations echo Theodore Roosevelt's notable proposition that "unless we keep the barbarian virtues, gaining the civilized ones will be of little avail' (quoted in Healy, 115).

The atavism of the new right-wing ideologues like Lord resides some way apart from the theocratic ideologies of revolutionary Islam. But much is shared: a cultural antagonism to modernity, a bewailing of the loss of older virtues, a taste for authoritarian leadership, a phallocratic and hierarchical view of social relations, and so on. The difference, as I've tried to say, between the two atavisms is essentially in the position from which they are articulated: if the peoples of the Arab world "suffer" from consumerism, the antimodernists of the North are by contrast the agents of its propagation. If for al-Qaida the remedy for suffering is the extirpation of capitalist interests and the installation of an atavistic religious sense, for the atavists of the North the answer is a moral and censorious disdain and the promotion of charismatic and authoritarian leadership. Thus the world is caught up not so much in the much-touted "clash of civilizations" (in Samuel Huntington's phrase, which has been popularized into a reductive watchword for the present moment); and perhaps it is not even the clash of barbarisms to which Gilbert Achcar imputes responsibility for the "new world disorder." Rather, it might be best described as a clash of atavisms, produced, in Freud's notable formulation, by the narcissism of small differences.

# *primitive accumulation*

*i* have been using the idea of atavism as a way of pointing to another variation on capital's theme, so to speak, whereby the primitive is structured into the progressiveness of this politico-economic system. The Retort group talks in similar terms when they suggest that a mixture of "atavism and new-fangledness" characterizes the current moment (186). For them, the "new-fangledness" is epitomized by what might be called mediatized capitalism—a phrase that would designate the ever-expanding capacities of the media and communication technologies in spectacularizing capitalism and globalizing both production and consumption. The atavism they speak of, dialectically bound up with the "new-fangledness," designates the continual rehearsal of capital's basic modes and habits. Retort identifies the process of primitive accumulation as perhaps the most important or trenchant among those modes.

In Marx's writing, primitive accumulation is the name given to the prehistory of capitalism itself, a period of expropriation and accumulation of property, land, and money, all of which will then be put to service in a properly instituted capitalist process. A crucial component of this period of accumulation is the removal of producers from their means of production—the removal of peasants from agricultural land, for instance—to establish a new regime of wage relations: "The capitalist system presupposes the complete separation of the laborers from all property in the means by which they can realize their labor" (*Capital* 1: 737–38).

So primitive accumulation is a kind of originary gesture for capitalism, equivalent to the "previous accumulation" posited by Adam Smith. But whereas Smith consigns it to some unexamined past moment, Marx tries to give the concept some historical flesh. He locates the beginning of the period of primitive accumulation at the end of the fiftheenth century with the "forcible driving of the peasantry from the land . . . and the usurpation of the common lands" (*Capital* 1: 434). This mechanism continued for two centuries across Europe: "The different moments of primitive accumulation can be assigned in particular to Spain, Portugal, Holland, France and England in more or less chronological order. These different moments are systematically combined together at the end of the seventeenth century in England" (*Capital* 1: 775–76). And these processes continue through to the nineteenth century. The central feature of those processes consisted in the dispossession of the peasantry, causing "a mass of free proletarians [to be] hurled onto the labour market" (*Capital* 1: 741) and permitting the conversion of both productive capacity and labor itself to the needs of capital.

For Marx, then, primitive accumulation is in essence the long history of the transition from feudalism to capitalism, a history of centuries and, as he remarks, a history to be "written in the annals of humanity in characters of fire and blood" (*Capital* 1: 738). "Capital," Marx says, "arrives dripping from head to toe, from every pore, with blood and dirt" (*Capital* 1: 899). Famously, he likens the role of primitive accumulation in capitalist development to the role of original sin in Christian theology and, on the face of it, it seems unarguable that, in *Capital* at least, Marx consigns primitive accumulation to a time before capitalism proper; it is part of capital's prehistory, and "not the result of the capitalist mode of production but its starting point"—however historically lengthy that point might have been (*Capital* 1: 736).

America, of course, has its own history of primitive accumulation, different from that of Europe, though equally long and bloody. Capital develops in relation to previous modes of production, as Marx shows, but American economic development lacks an organic relation to previous modes of production. For the American colonists, the land on the new continent was all seen as expropriable. Thus the first stage of primitive accumulation in America was the theft of land from Native Americans and the claiming of unused land. The agricultural base necessary for the development of industrial capital was initiated by this initial set of appropriations, and in the meantime the commercial and financial activities of what would become the United States could begin the construction of capital proper without having to overthrow or make a transition from another developed mode of production. The tensions between agricultural production and commerce and finance that in Europe had characterized the early development of capital were initially allayed in the American case by the need for a united front against the British, but the opening of the frontier began the process (culminating in the Civil War) whereby capital and agriculture came into conflict. The history of the frontier in the nineteenth century is, evidently, a fully formed part of America's mythographic heritage by now, but it also constitutes a unique phase of primitive accumulation. The continuous expansion of the nation, driven by the building of new railroads in the 1840s and the discovery of gold in California, through to the Homestead Act in 1862, constituted a period of accelerated expropriation.

In Michel Aglietta's words, the opening of the frontier "unleashed an extraordinary wave of speculation, plunder and monopolization of land by every available means of violence" (75). Even the briefest account that could be given of this "prehistory" of American capital would necessarily include at least the genocide of Native Americans and the theft or fraudulent expropriation of their land, the seizure of Mexican land and a war against Mexico, the sacrifice of immigrants to the struggle between railroad and mining corporations and the agricultural sector, many decades of the use of slavery and indentured servitude, and a bloody civil war. Even though America experienced what Aglietta calls "the ideal economic conditions for capitalism to take hold in the new economic spaces" (75) and even in the absence of any previous or established modes of production that needed to be swept away, the American phase of primitive accumulation was sufficiently horrific.

So, the "letters of fire and blood" of primitive accumulation are there to be read, in America as much as elsewhere, as the signs of capitalism's "starting point." But many debates have arisen about the term, raising the question of whether primitive accumulation really is simply part of capital's prehistory, or whether it continues throughout capitalist development. As Michael Perelman shows, Marx himself at different moments and in different writings at least hints at an ongoing role for the process (25–37). Certainly, for many Marxist writers, primitive accumulation persists beyond a merely transitional phase. Rosa Luxemburg, for example, saw primitive accumulation as a necessary force in capitalism's continued expansion around the globe and, in all its bloodiness, as a crucial component in capitalism's "barbarism":

> Yet capital in power performs the same task [of expropriation] even today, and on an even more important scale by modern colonial policy. It is an illusion to hope that capitalism will ever be content with the means of production which it can acquire by way of commodity exchange. In this respect already, capital is faced with difficulties because vast tracts of the globe's surface are in the possession of social organizations that have no desire for commodity exchange or cannot, because of the entire social structure and the forms of ownership, offer for sale the productive forces in which capital is primarily interested. . . . Capital must begin by planning for the systematic destruction and annihilation of all the non-capitalist social units which obstruct its development. With that we have passed beyond the stage of primitive accumulation; this process is still going on. (350)

The ninety or more years since Luxemburg wrote this have ensured that there are no longer "vast tracts" of the world untouched by capitalist expansion, and this mere fact can perhaps be taken as confirmation of her argument. Indeed, by now most Marxist writers seem to recognize some role for primitive accumulation beyond capital's prehistory. While mentioning an extended debate on the topic on *The Commoner* Web site (http://www.commoner.org.uk), David Harvey in *The New Imperialism* (2003) bypasses the theoretical niceties, simply proposing that, instead of primitive accumulation, one should talk of modern forms of plunder and dispossession. Other commentators are more attentive to the term itself. Michael Perelman, for example, argues that primitive accumulation does indeed continue throughout capital's history, that it is crucially part of the idea of accumulation per se, and that it serves as an especially useful concept for examining the development of the division of labor. Jason Read suggests that, while there is some question about "whether primitive accumulation can simply be relegated to the past or to the simple prehistory of the capitalist mode of production as a moment of transition," it seems feasible to suggest that primitive accumulation does in fact "encompass both the conditions for the historical formation of capital and its extension into other spaces and other modes of production" (26). Indeed, Read goes on to make the more extensive claim that "primitive accumulation becomes not only a cause of the capitalist mode of production but also its effect" (27).

One can perhaps say that primitive accumulation indeed persists throughout capitalism's history and is a particularly accurate term, as Luxemburg suggested, for what happens under colonial expansion and, now in the postcolonial period, under the aegis of globalization. The removal of native peoples and the expropriation of land in the Amazonian rainforest, the privatization of the commons in all parts of the world (including, of course, the United States), the forcible expropriation of the whole of Afghanistan or Iraq and the delivery of their means of production to private capitalist hands—any of these examples attests to the persistence of the methods of primitive accumulation and also, in most cases, to the force and violence needed to accomplish capital's goals. And each of the examples confirms in its way Marx's own reference to capital's "expropriating the final residue of direct producers who still have something left to expropriate" (*Grundrisse*, 348).

So it can be allowed that primitive accumulation and its accompanying violence and bloodiness continue at least as what Silvia Federici, in a fascinating account of the place of women in primitive accumulation, calls a return:

> A return of the most violent aspects of primitive
> accumulation has accompanied every phase of capitalist
> globalization, including the present one, demonstrating
> that the continuous expulsion of farmers from the land,
> war and plunder on a world scale, and the degradation
> of women are necessary conditions for the existence of
> capitalism in all times. (12–13)

Similarly, according to the Retort group, the post–9/11 scenario affords capitalism the opportunity to revivify the flagging economic fortunes of globalization by conducting "a new round of primitive accumulation" (36).

At the same time, it seems important to make the analytical distinction between the actual acts of dispossession and expropriation that constitute primitive accumulation and the purposes and consequences of those acts. This, in my view, is why Marx frequently appears content to consign primitive accumulation to the prehistory of capital: he is interested in making that distinction, unlike many contemporary commentators (Harvey, for instance), for whom the act of dispossession is certainly a moral and political outrage, but who don't follow through the analysis that Marx can offer. For Marx, in my understanding, there are two particular things to consider: first, in terms of the purpose of primitive accumulation, it is not only about the formation of capital and the making of a proletariat; equally important is the mobilization and circulation of capital. Primitive accumulation in that sense enables capital not just to form, but to "posit the conditions of its own realization" (*Grundrisse,* 459). Crucial among those conditions is the ability of capital—inchoate or fully fledged capital—to circulate. That is, capitalism is impelled to combat all noncapitalist forms and convert all noncapitalist places, not just for the sake of accumulation per se, but equally for the sake of circulation. As the world has seen in the U.S. invasions of Afghanistan and Iraq—wars of privatization, they might be called—the act of primitive accumulation itself is in a broader sense intended to remove obstacles to the free circulation of capital around the globe; to unblock, as it were, the clogged arteries that both those nations constituted in capital's circulatory system.

The second issue here—the matter of the immediate consequences of the act of dispossession or expropriation—concerns the universal imposition of the wage relation. It seems to me that it is necessary to distinguish theft and the forcible seizure of property and resources from the actual imposition of capital's specific kind of wage markets. Marx considered such imposition to be the necessary consequence of, or the necessary step following, acts of expropriation. In other words, there is a compulsory channeling of subjects into capital's wage-labor relation caused directly by the expropriation of resources. Again, the case of Iraq can provide a contemporary example. The invasion and overthrow of the Saddam Hussein regime enabled the wholesale privatization of the nation's means of production. This in turn forced Iraqis into a new set of social relations where the capitalist market dictates the terms of existence by turning Iraqi subjects into laborers for capital, "free" to sell their labor. This is the "silent compulsion" that Marx pointed to as the very thing that "sets the seal on the domination of the capitalist" (*Capital* 1: 761). In the months and years since the initial invasion, the upshot of this has become clear in the many reports and images of Iraqis who are unable to find employment and unable to accommodate themselves to the conditions of the new market regime and, what follows, a brand new class society.

My point here is to suggest why it might actually matter, especially right now, to consider the role of primitive accumulation in contemporary, globalized capitalism. It's not simply a matter of assuring fidelity to Marx or of cleaving to some proper theoretical line. The question, more exactly, is a matter of being able to describe the current moment, or the current state of the mode of production, with some specificity. The invasions and occupations of Afghanistan and Iraq have been repeatedly explained in terms that more or less absolutely elide the politico-economic realities that underpin them. Instead of expropriation, the world is told of liberation; instead of class struggle and anticapitalist sentiment, the world is told of religiously motivated insurgency; and so on. These American-led adventures in primitive accumulation underline the fact that modern forms of plunder do exist, but that the "original sin" of expropriation is only the half of it. The expropriations and dispossessions are part of ongoing processes of capital (and in the current moment, they can perhaps be seen as yet another means for fending off capital's crises of overproduction, as classic European imperialism was) whereby blockages in the global circulation of capital are cleared and capital's wage relation is imposed. Such an imposition is a permanent requirement of capitalism and necessitates that capitalism in a sense always has to return to its own prehistory. Contemporary primitive accumulation is *primitive* in the sense that it harks back to capital's beginnings, but it is no longer historically *prior*. Rather, it is a crucial component in the dialectic of the primitive and the modern, the barbaric and the civilized, within capitalism today.

# *imperial power*

*A*merica's experience of primitive accumulation, under what Aglietta calls "the ideal economic conditions for capitalism to take hold" (75), revolved crucially around both the ideological concept and the material reality of the frontier. The supposedly endless possibilities for capitalism's expansion across the continent obviously constituted, and still constitute, a significant imaginary for American life. Indeed, as Aglietta says, in the nineteenth century, "expansion became the dominant phenomenon in American life; it could almost be identified with the country's history" (74). But after the Civil War, the expansionist urge turned rather quickly to the frontier beyond American borders and thus to imperialism—a process whose beginnings in the 1890s were magisterially tracked by William Appleman Williams and a bit more recently by David Healy. From the 1890s through to the Vietnam War, it was not at all uncommon to hear American foreign policy described as "imperial." The lengthy and bloody debacle of the Vietnam War was, clearly, the culminating moment of this supposed American imperialism, and the end of that war seemed to mark some sort of retreat from overt imperial ambition.

Since 9/11, however, there has been an apparently unstoppable re-emergence of the terms *imperialism* and *empire* to describe the situation of the United States. One might have expected that thinkers on the left (and more specifically, Marxist thinkers) would have been largely responsible for this rhetorical fashion. The current climate, however, is such that the terms *imperialism* and *empire* have become almost shibboleths in all corners of public discourse. Columnists like Sebastian Mallaby in *The Washington Post* (May 10, 2004) have unabashedly argued for the proper application of a reinvigorated and benign American imperialism, picking up on a trend that Niall Ferguson's *Colossus: The Price of American Empire* (2004) had some responsibility for popularizing. Reviews in publications like the *New York Times* and the *Washington Post* pulled together large numbers of books on the rights and wrongs of the American imperium, while *The Nation* magazine in 2003 managed to find thirteen books to review that specifically invoked American empire, from the right, the left, and the center. What Ferguson derides as the "anguished tones" (3) of objection to American imperialism emanated, of course, from people like Noam Chomsky on the left and from liberals like Chalmers Johnson, for whom American empire has an unbroken history stretching back to the early nineteenth century (2004). But leftists and liberals held no copyright on the word, which was—and is—everywhere. Indeed, a rather comic reminder of the fact was recently supplied by a group of jejune California graduate students: announcing a new journal that would be open to every kind of cutting-edge scholarship, they banned material on American empire because that topic has already been done to death.

The flooding of the word *imperialism* into the mainstream is perhaps a little surprising—though it does clearly derive from and reflect the more generally unapologetic rhetoric and brazen confidence of the neoconservative ideologues gathered in the Bush administrations. More surprising, perhaps, is the fact that the left—once the unchallenged owners of the term—has been slow to get abreast. Or perhaps this isn't so surprising when one considers that less than a decade ago—indeed, for the past two decades—Marxist theories of imperialism appeared exhausted or dormant, and little work had been done to revivify them. In the late 1950s, Paul Baran, with his *Political Economy of Growth,* had overturned many of the methodological assumptions of Marxism to account for the kind of imperialism he saw in the United States at that time, spearheaded by the growth of transnational corporations and subvented by massive military spending. And Baran's work was followed by a decade or so of discussion about the question of imperialism, provoked in large part by America's adventure in Vietnam; Harry Magdoff's trenchant writing (such as *The Age of Imperialism* [1969]) was central at that time. But in recent decades, Marxist work has tended to concentrate on dependency theory and various definitions and analyses of the postcolonial situation, almost as if imperialism itself were a dead letter. Much work of that stripe also implied or assumed, as Anthony Brewer wrote in 1989 that "U.S. hegemony in the capitalist world is clearly over" (273) and thus it rather readily made way for theories of globalization that often wishfully proclaimed, like Michael Howard and John

King, that "a fully capitalized world [was], therefore, a less imperialist world" (37).

One observer in the mid-1990s, Richard McIntyre, pointed up the absence of Marxist theories of imperialism in the last decades of the twentieth century and suggested that imperialism as a major theoretical concern and focus had been overtaken by the new intellectual concerns of cultural studies, poststructuralism, multiculturalism, and the like—and indeed imperialism itself had been obviated by the changing historical conjuncture (the Gulf War, the new world order, the end of history, the process of globalization, and so on). A measure of the correctness of the observation is that his comment appears as one of less than a handful of references to imperialism in a huge 1995 collection edited by Antonio Callari called *Marxism in the Postmodern Age: Confronting the New World Order.*

The rather schematic and perhaps rote nature of McIntyre's account should not be allowed to obscure his essential point. Even during the Gulf War itself, or before that with the various displays of American aggression in the Reagan era, the word *imperialism* seemed absent without leave from most scholarly and journalistic discourse, appearing with some frequency only in the street-corner newsprint of the far left. It seems that the term retained little charge for the analysis of a world situation characterized by the relatively peaceable spread of consumer goods, the increasing hypermobility of capital, and the vexed but steady growth of supranational cooperation and institutions—the time, in short, of the processes known as globalization. Even David Harvey, whose recent proclamation of the "New Imperialism" epitomizes the revival of the term, had previously written extensively on the globalization process in the 1990s without registering much of an imperial dimension.

For all that, it might be less than glibly commonsensical to suggest that globalization has been the continuation of imperialism by other means. There has, however, been very little work that has explicitly set out to prove such a proposition. Far too often—even on the left—analysis has been complicit with the mainstream insistence on the *rupture* that globalization ostensibly makes with previous forms of capitalist relations. There are exceptions, of course, and among them one would note the tireless effort of Samir Amin to show that the discourse of globalization constitutes "an ideological discourse used to legitimize the strategies of the imperialist capital that dominates the current phase" and to argue that "the form of globalization depends . . . on the class struggle" (158). But by and large, it is true to say that the discourse of globalization has more often than not served as an alibi for forgetting the features of fundamentalist capitalism, either in regard to imperial expansion or to the more generalized extension of the wage relation that it clearly depends on.

Certainly, it has been the effort of most public discourse to completely deny such fundaments, and much scholarly and policy work has gone along with this. Consequently, the least that can be said is that the public relations image of globalization has managed to remain much less tarnished than the image of imperialism, even while available understanding of globalization in relation to imperialism has remained scant. Even after the return of imperialism as an analytical category, many commentators still do not make the link between imperialism and globalization, preferring to see it as yet another rupture (that is, the new imperialism as an interruption of globalization), or as a kind of intensification of the processes of globalization. Jan Nederveen Pieterse, for an extreme example, sees imperialism as only part of a huger and longer process of globalization, thus elevating globalization to the prime position of analysis.

There are exceptions to this dreary scenario, of course, and perhaps the most visible attempt to conceptualize the connection between imperialism and globalization has been Michael Hardt and Antonio Negri's bestseller, *Empire* (2000). Hardt and Negri argue that globalization induces a kind of sea change in capitalist relations, where the power of nation-states is displaced by what they call Empire, a globalized network of decentralized or deterritorialized economic and cultural relationships. In its displacement of political power by economic and cultural power, this Empire constitutes a break from classic imperialism (which had depended on the extension of political power from a given nation to another). Empire is thence explicitly constructed as coeval with globalization and antithetical in all relevant ways to the

European and American instances of imperialism and colonialism in the nineteenth and twentieth centuries.

Hardt and Negri see this decentered and deterritorializing Empire as sowing the seeds of its own putative destruction by producing multifarious resistances and antagonistic desires among the "multitudes." That vision, combined with a recommendation for some supranational tutelary institutions (embracing a form of constitutionalism that must have come as something of a surprise to their readers on the left) looked good enough in the late 1990s to satisfy the postmodernist conviction that even so totalizing a phenomenon as globalization itself would not require analysis by way of the old "totalizing" habits and language of Marxism. Thus, the publication of *Empire* became a big event for the liberal intelligentsia and postmodernists everywhere. But the claims of *Empire*—and by extension, many similar claims revolving around a faith in the historical *rupture* produced by (or *as*) globalization—have surely taken quite a knock from the very events that have by now presumably consigned the book to the remainder piles. That is, the American response to the vicious antiglobalization protest that we now refer to as 9/11 has arguably given the lie to the kinds of claims that Hardt and Negri make at the beginning of their book, where they italicize the proposition that "[t]he United States does not, and indeed no nation-state can today, form the centre of an imperialist project. Imperialism is over" (xiv). The subjugation of Afghanistan, the extraordinary assault on Iraq, and the cynical and botched occupations of both—these events have at least muddied the waters for such a case. And indeed, these are the very same events that have occasioned the sudden revival of the term *imperialism* itself, not just in Marxist or leftist discourse, but pretty much everywhere.

The identification and discussion of a new American imperialist project is reminiscent of the 1960s, when the most recondite scholarly and theoretical discourse, as well as the most vernacular and populist discourses, regularly deployed the term and gauged its relevance to the depredations of U.S. foreign policy. And indeed it might well be that the memory of Vietnam—a fraught cultural signifier in America even now, thirty years on, and one that has explicitly and avowedly driven the thinking of parts of the American right for decades—is sufficient to explain the revival of the term. (Certainly at the time of the invasion of Iraq, there was no shortage of discussion around the question of whether Iraq was to become Bush's Vietnam.) But the discussions of imperialism that took place in the Vietnam era hardly ever took the term for granted. It's true that the vernacular use of the term at that time often threatened to render it so vague as to be almost useless, but by the same token, even journalistic and certainly scholarly uses attempted to make distinctions and forge definitions based on the various traditions of defining imperialism—most notably, of course, the Marxist tradition, with its classic readings from Bukharin and Lenin. We might well be in danger at the moment of returning to the vaguer use of the term, but the better hope is that even the loosest vernacular understanding of imperialism could well be the impulse needed to help revive the concept and drive some new analysis. This seems particularly important after so much focus on the processes of globalization per se, and even more so when globalization itself has so often been understood in terms that echo Hardt and Negri and their "decentering" of political processes.

Hardt and Negri rather disingenuously enlist Lenin's work on imperialism in the genealogy of their new "Empire" (234)—even though their own idea of "Empire" more closely resembles Karl Kautsky's vision of an "ultra-imperialism" that Lenin spent so many pages dismantling. And indeed, in their later work, *Multitude* (2004), Hardt and Negri creep even closer to Kautsky's view of imperialism by reproducing almost exactly Kautsky's argument that at the time of World War I, that conflict was antithetical to the economic interests of business. *Multitude* confronts post–9/11 American military action with the parallel claim that such action is counterproductive, rationally antithetical to capitalist interests. Instead of committing acts of coercive domination, the United States would do better to cooperate with other international actors and organizations because this would sit more comfortably with what they see as the aims of Empire: "In order to maintain itself Empire must create a network form of power that does not isolate a center of control and excludes no outside lands or productive forces" (324).

Lenin, of course, construed his theories of imperialism largely as an antidote to what he thought of as Kautsky's reactionary and bourgeois-reformist turn of thought. Lenin was particularly scathing in his view of

Kautsky's notions of an "ultra-imperialism," where the dangers of inter-imperialist rivalries might be obviated by "the joint exploitation of the world by internationally united finance capital" (261). And Lenin's dismissal of Kautsky, whom he accused of misleading the masses with his theory (261–62), might be usefully noted by those who are seduced by Hardt and Negri's championing of multitudes and their "acts of love" against Empire (351).

Lenin's own main intervention consisted in his deviation from the traditional view of imperialism as simply the expansion and exploitation of dominated territories. Rather, his approach is fundamentally and avowedly economistic, making imperialism the necessary consequence of competition between the colonizing capitalist powers at a moment when financial capital was coming to dominate productive capital. For Lenin, the central mechanism of imperialism is the export of capital in an "international network of dependence and ties," leading to the "formation of international capitalist monopolies which share the world among themselves" (237). Lenin is clear that the imperialism he is talking about is a special case, a particular historical phenomenon within the development of capitalism, predicated on the dominance of financial capital and thus on the needs of capital circulation. That indeed is the strength of his position—a trenchantly empirical historicizing of early twentieth-century colonialism and imperialism. But that very strength also makes the analysis less than perfect for understanding later imperial scenarios. As capital develops, the peculiar circumstances that underpin its forms inevitably change, and the economic forms in particular change as capital makes and remakes itself. Indeed, for Michel Aglietta, the very nature of imperialism is misconceived through a primarily economic perspective like Lenin's. For Aglietta, such a "reductively economistic perspective . . . distorts [imperialism's] significance. There is hardly a domain in which unswerving fidelity to Lenin has been more damaging" (29).

Part of the theoretical damage is to be seen in the simple equation of imperialism with colonialism that still underpins much thinking about imperialism and where the mechanisms of capital export, territorial possession, and resource extraction are said to go irretrievably hand in hand. The current conjuncture does not seem to square with a

amentalist or primitive
capital, and concomi-
d the "subject of value,"
abled according to the
nent. Importantly here,
ucture—that has effec-
ight from Gramsci's day
course, the successful
ds the establishment of
conditions in different
ies in the development

the pertinence of the
the structuring of the
ization. The fundamen-
—and indeed, its symp-
inequalities and other
nore visible on a world
rrors so severe as think-
ection, or as some kind
t the prime directive of
cate discussion of class,
ourse functions to dis-
s division within north-
pt perhaps in the hugely
ld" doublet permits.
atory efforts of the ide-
t, or in the liberal resis-
l Negri talk about their
l capitalist procedures,
only by a prior evacua-
e relation. In *Multitude*,
bor that makes suppos-
nformation, communi-
"—and suggest that the
bor theory of value. It's

clear that they have been seduced by the ideas of the right-wing cheer-leaders for globalization, who from very early on suggested that global-ization had brought about a change in the system of value production such that it would no longer be labor that produced value, but rather knowledge. I've discussed those early globalizing ideologies at length in my *Millennial Dreams,* and like many others, I have pointed out the sleight of hand involved in that kind of proposition. The simple empir-ical fact is that the wage relation has not changed, even if the nature of labor's product has changed. Capitalism is in fact almost wholly indifferent to the precise nature of the commodity, so long as there re-mains some kind of commodity to facilitate the circulation of capital. Be they "symbolic analysts," as Robert Reich called them a decade ago, or "knowledge workers" as Peter Drucker called them, or "immaterial laborers," as Hardt and Negri's trendy phrase now belatedly calls them, workers in any industry still stand in relation to capital in pretty much the way that Marx describes. In other words, it's less the nature of the product that defines labor and more the fact that laborers sell their time to capital in the wage relation.

It is this basic structure of the wage relation that the interstate im-perialist system attempts to instantiate in all corners of the globe. That is why I have been stressing the view that, in Aglietta's terms, any analy-sis of imperialism must begin with an analysis of asymmetrical inter-state relations, the way those relations are established and maintained, and how, at the economic level, they have "their roots in the most gen-eral determinants of the wage relation" (30–31). In this view, today's imperialism is thus an interstate political mechanism for the general extension of capital's wage relation across a global space, and it seems less and less like a classic colonial enterprise. In that sense, the oppor-tunistic subjugation of Iraq is no doubt a *symptom* of imperialist desire, or more exactly a demonstration of it. But the desire and the actuality of imperialism in the twenty-first century is best understood as some-thing larger than any individual action of the United States, in Iraq or elsewhere. Indeed, the notion of "American imperialism" is almost pleonastic, since the United States, as a central player in this system for the expansion of capitalist production, is always already imperialist by dint of the nature of that system.

occupation, and "recon-
lonialist-imperialist busi-
ecome revived right now.
out specific resources, as
iagining; from that point
even the first Gulf War
tions of the Leninist cat-
perialist conjuncture that
d motives underlying the
lestroy Saddam Hussein's
e land or resources.
Leninist definition of im-
ation than any other cur-
grasped on the basis of a
state relations" (32). That
ied, of course, as a purely
peaks a "complex form of
non Bromley has pointed
orm of socialization had
zation. Bromley uses that
cian way, to point to the
include. Gramsci writes:

ıment, a
termined
f State. The
of free-trade
out in the more
f economic
on the level of
nent, itself
tion and
)

e processes whereby the
he everyday life of U.S.

If the classic Leninist view is of imperialism as a necessary consequence of economic competition among the colonialist capitalist powers,
leading to colonial violence and war between the capitalist protagonists,
then, as I've suggested above, we at least have to recognize the historical specificity of that description. Aglietta's view of the contemporary transnational system suggests that imperialism today is *built in,*
as it were, to the activity of that system. Within that activity there is
no longer the kind of Leninist competition between states that led to
war and violence, but rather a much less antagonistic struggle between
powers, a struggle to forge political hegemony or leadership within an
interstate, globalized context. According to Aglietta, this would be a
"hegemony . . . through which one state manages to influence a series
of other states to adopt a set of rules that are favourable to the stability
of a vast space of multilateral commodity relations guaranteeing the
circulation of capital" (32).

Such a struggle for hegemony or leadership is always both economic
*and* political, where both processes are dedicated to the continuation of
the circulation of capital. There are many consequences once we agree
to such a shift in the analytical frame. Not least among these would be
the need for a specification of the globalized or interstate economic situation in a way equivalent to Lenin's account of early twentieth-century
colonialism-imperialism. Such a description would no doubt include
some account of the diminution of America's economic leadership at
the same time as its military superiority came to be apparently unchal-
lengeable. But equally, such a shift in emphasis would demand a description of the interstate system that recognizes the function it serves as
guarantor of capital's circulation at the same time that it examines the
peculiar and changing politics of the global system.

The principal feature of this interstate system, then, is that it is, in
and of itself, imperialist. It is a transnational mechanism designated to
socialize the world into capitalist relations of production and consumption. Yet the capitalist powers that motivate that system also struggle
for influence, for advantage, and for the role of leadership. Among the
imperialist powers, in other words, there is both antagonism and coordination. In Simon Bromley's account of this struggle, there are two
principal dimensions of the exercise of power: the coercive and the

cooperative. On the one hand is coercive power, whereby one region gets everyone else to agree to its ways; but on the other is collective power, where cooperative strategies work for common goals.

The two dimensions could be seen in play in an almost cartoonish way in the 2004 U.S. presidential election campaign, with Bush arguing that the United States should rely on its coercive power to assert its predominant role over the other imperialist powers and John Kerry arguing for a strategy of greater cooperation with and among those powers. Part of the dismal falsity of the debate and the election itself resided in the claim that there was indeed a choice to be made between the two strategies, in a way that was reminiscent of the well-known beer commercial, where consumers are given a choice between two qualities of the same beer (great taste, less filling). In fact, the two dimensions are operatively inseparable since the smooth functioning, or the delicate equilibrium, of the interstate imperialist system depends on coordination and cooperation as much as on any individual state's actions. In this sense, the current imperialist system conducts itself more in the way that Marx described than in the way Lenin described. Even the exercise of force by the United States in Afghanistan and Iraq has worked for the collaborative benefit of the system, forming what Bromley describes as new "states and economies . . . successfully co-coordinated with the rest of the capitalist world, rather than a prize to be won by the United States at the expense of rival core imperialisms. It is imperialism but it is not, primarily, inter-imperialist rivalry" (61).

At the same time, there is no point in denying that whatever equilibrium might have existed in this interstate system was rudely shaken up by the Bush administration's policies and actions since 9/11. But the path taken—however much it has provoked the use of the term "U.S. imperialism" in the ways we have seen—can ultimately be understood as an egregious and badly judged intervention designed largely to reconsolidate American hegemony in the system, a hegemonic position that had been slipping for a number of years. Essentially the Bush administration's warmongering has been an opportunistic exercise of U.S. military power in a context where U.S. political and economic power had been waning. That is, the attacks of 9/11 presented the administration with the occasion to bypass the collaborative mechanisms of the international order and trump them by the assertion of U.S. military dominance.

It is no doubt this peremptory disregard for the standing international order that explains most of the anger and opposition from the imperialist co-players, such as the European Union. The European Union (as well as its components parts), Russia, and even Japan and China now are the most immediate co-players with the United States in the imperialist system. In that light, the acute disagreements that marked the onset of the Iraq invasion can be no surprise, since the American action produced a major disturbance in the relative equilibrium in this system between distributive or coercive power and co-operative power. Indeed, one way of describing the American determination to ride roughshod over all other international interests in and objections to the Iraqi invasion is to point again to Aglietta's notion of the need to forge a hegemonic position within the contemporary system of states. In that light, the invasion of Iraq can be seen less as a preemptive assault against a dangerous and threatening foe, and more as a preemption of the other powers in the imperial system, whose acceptance of the rules of the collaborative game was simply derided by the American posture.

Alongside the Bush administration's willingness to alienate its imperialist co-players, the most remarkable (and remarked upon) component of the American flouting of rules and standards was the treatment of the United Nations and other supranational organizations and entities. The fundamentalists of U.S. culture (both political and cultural ones) have long despised the UN and other such supranational entities, seeing them as a threat to U.S. sovereignty and preferring to apply the logic of the free market to political dealings as well as economic ones. Yet the UN, NATO, international nuclear and environmental treaties, the G8 with its control over international financial exchange, the Organization for Economic Co-operation and Development, the World Trade Organization and the World Bank, and a plethora of other, more minor nongovernmental organizations—all these institutions and organizations normally have a place in the ongoing operation of the interstate system that constitutes contemporary imperialism. And all of them appeared, in one way or another, as mere pawns in a game that the United

States was intent on winning after 9/11. Such organizations help in various ways to coordinate the activities and aims of the various imperialist powers. An older view from the left might claim that they act merely as the brokers for the claims and ambitions of competing powers. And certainly there is plenty of ammunition for the kind of charge that Tariq Ali makes about the UN when he assails Kofi Annan for his "role as a dumb-waiter for American aggression" during the run-up to the Iraq invasion (12). But it perhaps makes just as much sense to see such organizations as intended to prevent, precisely, the development of the kind of vicious imperialist competition that has led to war and violence. It is for that reason, if for no other, that we still have to insist on the positive function (even if not the efficacy) of all the so-called supranational institutions that attend the imperialist system and that have appeared compromised and confused in the face of Bush's renewal of U.S. dominance.

It is, at any rate, the case that the intense international disagreements and disputes witnessed in the run-up to the U.S. war against Iraq in no way contradict the existence of broad common interests among the imperialist nations and groups. My point here has been to say that this was not so much a struggle between competing imperialist powers as a kind of constitutional crisis in the collaborative mechanisms of the interstate system, provoked by the willingness of the U.S. administration to throw away the rule book. This crisis, then, was less a classic national imperialist venture by the United States and more a new moment in the continual struggle for hegemony, where the United States pulled out rather more stops than usual by making a straightforward bid for outright dominance. Nonetheless, what remains beneath the disagreements is a solidarity of interest: the general extension of capitalist wage relations across the world, the concomitant free circulation of capital, and the promotion of both from within an interstate system that is itself imperialist, and in which the United States tried to assert uncontestable leadership.

If we take all of this to be the structure of contemporary imperialism, the claim of Hardt and Negri quoted earlier—"The United States does not, and indeed no nation-state can today, form the center of an imperialist project. Imperialism is over."—is even less sustainable after the Iraq invasion than it was when they uttered it. The attacks of 9/11 were direct strikes against the beating heart of capital, the symbolic center of capital's circulatory system, as David Harvey makes clear, and the American "response," as is now widely acknowledged, has been only marginally—or simply rhetorically—related to either a retaliatory or a preemptive war on terror and "rogue" states. More fundamentally, the attacks of 9/11 produced the occasion for the United States to do two things: first, to attack Afghanistan and Iraq and thereby free up two blocked arteries in the circulatory system of twenty-first-century capitalism; and second, to reassert its hegemonic role in the system of states. However much difficulty the United States has had in effecting those projects, they are firmly rooted in the structure of today's imperialism.

The general point is perhaps reinforced by the fact that the newly asserted dominance of the United States has remained problematic and contested, even after the the occupation of Iraq. The invasion was clearly a high-stakes gamble for the Bush administration, and it could be said that in many ways, the United States has paid dearly for it. The deaths of so many Iraqis and Americans, the continued violence and insurgencies, the scandals and ongoing suspicions about U.S. treatment of prisoners, the damage done to political relations around the world (and not just in the circle of imperialist powers), and the enormous financial burden the war has placed on U.S. resources—all these factors, and more, can be considered an exceptionally high price that the United States has paid for flouting the rules.

## meaningless politics

The view of contemporary imperialism that I have been putting forward here, though it rejects the Leninist shibboleths, still stipulates that imperialism is fundamentally a product of contemporary capitalist economic relations. Whether we call those economic relations globalization, neoimperialism, or some other name, the salient features are empirically the same: indisputably, capitalism is involved in extending its regime of wage relations everywhere around the globe, seeking also to free up any blocked arteries in the international circulation of capital, and resorting opportunistically and aggressively to whatever acts of dispossession present themselves. These are all points that I tried to make in my *Millennial Dreams* several years ago, as well as in the previous pages. That is, whatever the epiphenomenal changes occurring in capitalism's organization, the mode of production and its goals remain the same.

And yet, in relation to the newly rediscovered question of imperialism, so many commentators, from left to right and everywhere in between, continue to separate out the economic and the political aspects, stressing one in the absence of the other. One sterling exception is David Harvey's *The New Imperialism* (which invokes the debate over primitive accumulation that I have already considered). Harvey's analysis stresses the globalized processes of capital accumulation and circulation: globalization brings the increased concentration and accumulation of capital, along with, increasingly, both unfettered circulation (enhanced by technology and the protection of it) and extended forms of what Harvey calls accumulation by dispossession. For Harvey, the "imperial" global position of the United States is actually a contradiction, since U.S. hegemony in the world system is being permanently undermined by its economic weakness, such that the United States can maintain hegemony only through military superiority.

From his otherwise powerful analysis, however, Harvey reaches a rather strange conclusion. Faced with the contradiction between U.S. economic strength and its military strength, Harvey suggests that the logic of imperialism will eventually give way to the logic of capital itself:

> [T]he more it is realized that [the U.S. government] is
> currently dominated by a coalition of the military-
> industrial complex, neo-conservatives, and, even more
> worryingly, fundamentalist Christians, the more the logic
> of capital will look to regime change in Washington as
> necessary to its own survival. (207)

This rather optimistic proposition (conspicuously close to much older claims that violence and war were not in the interests of the capitalist) shows few signs yet of being played out. This is no doubt because the two "logics" cannot in the end be separated in the way that Harvey wants them to be. There is no reason to suppose that the interests of capital suffer from militarism, nor that the logic of imperialism will not lead to the reassertion of capitalist solidarity in the interstate system. Indeed, this was already beginning to happen in the first months of Bush's second term as the United States and the other imperial powers attempted a pragmatic reconciliation after the Iraqi war—and, notably, expressing their solidarity through concerted engagement with some of the remaining blocked arteries in capital's circulatory system, such as Iran, Syria, and North Korea. The rapprochement has been continued in various ways: the multinational operation to overthrow the elected government of Haiti in 2003, the international blind eye that was turned toward U.S. operations of illegal renditions and torture, the solidarity of "the international community" in the largely manufactured stand-off with Iran over its nuclear programs, and so on.

Harvey's belief that capital logic can eventually trump the new imperialism also needs to be complicated by the recognition of the powerful ideological component of the Bush administration's conduct. While Harvey is clearly aware of those ideological positions and critical of them, he nonetheless consistently underplays precisely their effect. It would be wrong, of course, to posit the administration's ideological urge as some sort of basic cause for economic fundamentalism and military action; but it would be equally dangerous to underestimate its simple ideological intransigence. The fact is, the current administration's commitment to ideological tenets is egregious—egregious in the sense that the desire and will to exercise a particular ideological program is arguably stronger than in any U.S. administration in the twentieth century. At the same time that it is anchored on the one side by being enmeshed in the imperialist system, this administration is anchored on the other by its extraordinary commitment to a doctrinaire ideological position.

If Harvey somewhat underplays that ideological commitment and the vehemence and elaborateness of the neoconservative agenda, other commentators will take it into account, but usually at the expense of any sense of the economic. One instance of this is the interesting work of Claes Ryn, who sees the ideological aspect of the current regime as the instantiation of what he calls a "new Jacobin ideology" resting on a highly elaborated sense of the essence of the virtues of America that are universal in appeal and can and should be applied everywhere. I'll say more about Ryn's view, but for the moment it's important to note that his treatment of the ideas and ideologies that rule the current administration's politics appear to have no relation to the economic realities that Harvey has attempted to explicate. For liberal thinkers like Ryn, it appears sufficient to explain political behaviors and programs as a function of ideological commitments, with no reference whatever to the interests of the fundamentalist capitalism that those politics eventually serve. But of course, the ideological, the political, and the economic cannot finally be separated out—still less can one aspect be taken to be finally determinate while the others are absent. This is the error that even so astute a commentator as Alain Touraine has made, with his proposal that "the principal logic of action of the president and his administration is political, military, and ideological," where the economic is apparently not worthy of mention (303).

However, Touraine's point—or his emphasis at least—is well taken in other respects. He argues that what enables the kind of modern interstate imperialism I have been pointing to is what he calls a "meaningless politics," where the political functions of contemporary northern states (and not just the United States) have become more and more disjunct from the social and civic responsibilities that the state has traditionally assumed in post-Enlightenment modernity. There are many ways of articulating this ever-growing disjuncture, or what we might call this erosion of civility. John Milbank, for instance, points out "the emptiness of the secular as such, and the consequent disguised sacralization of violence" in America (321). The evacuation of the secular has entailed virtually the complete elision of the kinds of associative and communitarian practices of the American past that were a crucial component in the dialectic of American civic life. These are the civic values and the same kind of political values and social organization cherished by William Appleman Williams: as against the purely commercial drive and desires of the republic, Williams consistently held out hope for the revival of a politics based in what can best be called communitarianism.

But this, of course, is exactly the kind of tradition that Milbank says "is today rarely able to achieve any conscious political articulation" (321).

In other words, the culture of modern democracies comes to be alienated from political processes. This tendency can only aid and abet the kind of internal or domestic changes in the United States that go hand in hand with the assertion of imperial hegemony. The symptoms are many and familiar, not least the decline in electoral participation that seems to afflict the United States. Or, as a related example, the overwhelming popular opposition to the Iraqi invasion in many northern democratic countries early in 2003 met with not much more than the deafness and defiance of the governments involved—the British, Italian, and Spanish, in particular—and their determination to subvent the interstate political project of the war. The increasingly corporatized and centralized media—precisely mediating the relationship between public and civic processes—have done much to elide or at least trivialize the link between the populace and the state, and at the same time to reproduce from their "embedded" positions predominantly official knowledge. These factors probably pale into insignificance compared with the damage done by what is now the norm in the northern democracies, but especially the United States: namely, the brokering of politics by corporate money and interests. Party political government in the North has been confirmed as a corporate activity, rather than a demotic one.

For Touraine, and for my purposes here, those kinds of phenomena can be seen as evidence of a contemporary dissolution of the links between the politics of the state, and not only the constituencies, but also the general social and cultural responsibilities of states. But here I want to go a bit further than Touraine (bleak as his analysis might already seem). On the one hand I think it is crucial, as I've suggested, to relocate Touraine's analysis into the economic frame of the general circulation of capital and capitalism's wage relation (rather than by merely topical reference to specific resources like oil, or to territorial possession per se); and on the other hand, it seems equally important to recognize the specificity of the current moment, especially insofar as it pertains to the United States.

# ideologues

*t*here has been in the United States since 9/11 a double strategy at work: not only an outward display of imperialist relations, but also an inward display of them. What I mean is that a crucial part of the international imperialism we now face is funded by the *deliberate* evacuation of the national democratic relation, and a *knowing* push toward authoritarianism, certainly within the United States. Indeed, it would not be outlandish to argue that Bush's "war on terror," the occupation of Afghanistan, and the sacking of Iraq should be understood as exactly the occasion and the opportunity for what was already the neoconservative ideological desire for a shift in the character of American culture. Just as the endless war serves the imperial system, keeping in line and attempting to corral nations and regions that are "out of line," so the ideological agenda's imperatives entail an increase in authoritarianism at home. In "Cracks in the Edifice of the Empire State," David Harvey recognizes this double movement as an "inner/outer dialectic" (212) suggesting that the currently empowered neoconservatives "intuitively accepted [Hannah] Arendt's view that empire abroad entails tyranny at home, but state it differently. Military activity abroad requires military-like discipline at home" (193). Harvey here shies away from suggesting that the United States needs to become authoritarian or totalitarian to conduct its endless war (and this is an issue I'll take up below), but it is clear enough by now that the administration's opportunistic reaction or response to 9/11 has not been confined to military and imperial policies. Rather, there has been a clear domestic project as well.

The desiderata of many of the protagonists in Bush's administration with regard to the "outer" part of this dialectic were all clearly laid out (and quite closely planned), long before the administration ever took power, in the Project for the New American Century (PNAC), whose pronouncements over the last few years have been readily available on the organization's Web site (www.newamericancentury.org) and by way of the separate publications of many of its members. It is perhaps a telling measure of the "embedded" state of mainstream American media that they have received less attention within the United States and are still less well-known here than elsewhere in the world. Given that the project was openly published, with signatories of great note, and given that it laid out in clear detail what turned out to be the Bush administration's path, and given that the project and its Web site continue, it's difficult to understand why PNAC has not become a centerpiece of media discussion.

PNAC's statement of principles, as expounded, for example, in a letter to President Clinton in 1998, recommends preemptive use of American forces around the world—and particularly in Iraq, where the aim would be to "eliminate the possibility that Iraq will be able to use or threaten to use weapons of mass destruction. In the near term, this means a willingness to undertake military action as diplomacy is clearly failing." For PNAC, however, the removal of Saddam Hussein's regime is not merely about weapons of mass destruction, just as the eventual war itself was not. For PNAC, regime change is also a necessary first step toward a broader strategic vision, for the Middle East and elsewhere. The thinking of PNAC often harks back to the golden age of Ronald Reagan's presidency, and in regard to the Middle East, it sees a prospect analogous to the collapse of Soviet power and the consequent reformation of many nations. The expansion and defense of freedom would rely on the ability of U.S. power "to shape circumstances before crises emerge, and to meet threats before they become dire. The history of this century should have taught us to embrace the cause of American leadership." The recommendations arising from this larger strategic vision include massively increasing defense spending, challenging perceived enemies, and promoting "freedom," thus encouraging a world more hospitable to "American values." PNAC's recommendations, including the doctrine of preemptive violence, quickly became enshrined as U.S. policy by way of the National Security Strategy early in 2002, which promised to "extend the benefits of liberty and prosperity through the spread of American values" (see www.whitehouse.gov/nsc/nss.html). It is noteworthy that the two mainsprings of the strategy articulated before 9/11—preemption of threats and the spreading of "freedom" and "democracy"—both in fact demand offensive, proactive tactics, and yet both have now been rationalized as essentially defensive responses to 9/11.

It is also worth remarking that PNAC's justification for calling for Hussein's removal rested at first largely on the perceived threat of weapons of mass destruction. On ABC's *Nightline* (March 10, 2003) William Kristol professed that he was certain the United States would be "vindicated when we discover the weapons of mass destruction and when we liberate the people of Iraq." But as with the administration itself, PNAC's response to the absence of those weapons in Iraq did not dampen enthusiasm for the war, since the invasion was only the first step in the broader strategy of making the world safe for American leadership. Once the war began, PNAC's rhetoric concentrated on the project of spreading freedom and democracy, in exactly the same way that administration rhetoric shifted in Bush's second term. Equally, the initial PNAC arguments in the late 1990s and into the first year of Bush's presidency were overtly predicated on the existence of large U.S. budget surpluses, which, PNAC proposed, should be used in defense spending. But the PNAC demand for increased defense spending far outlasted the availability of those surpluses, such that they could eventually only point to "an increasingly dangerous gap between our strategic ends and our military means, and the Bush Doctrine cannot be carried out effectively without a larger military force" (see http://www.newamericancentury.org/defense-20030123.htm).

Both of those principal predicates to PNAC's position have been more or less forgotten by now, and they have been replaced by the rush to what Ryn dubs "democratism," or what Bush has consistently called the "spread of freedom." That agenda predictably takes in much—but by no means all—of the Middle East. But recently PNAC has been paying much more attention to China as another obstacle to the spread of freedom, and this emphasis might be indicative of PNAC's ultimate and unstated concerns all along—the growing threat of a changing China to the interstate imperial system and its control of the world economy.

The majority of PNAC's members responsible for the original strategic calls were, or have by now been, placed in influential posts within the two Bush administrations. Dick Cheney, Donald Rumsfeld, and Paul Wolfowitz are probably the most visible and well known, but there are many others. Among the more influential are Cheney's former chief of staff, I. Lewis Libby, who is now better known for his indictment in

2005 by a special prosecutor for lying to a grand jury in the case of the leaking of the identity of CIA operative Valerie Plame; Aaron Friedberg, a professor who is now Cheney's Deputy National Security Adviser; the unspeakable Elliott Abrams, who, like several others in the Bush administrations, has been rehabilitated from the crimes for which he was convicted in the Iran-Contra conspiracy during the Reagan administration and who is now a presidential assistant and a deputy National Security Advisor; and John Bolton, who had been an undersecretary of state until he was controversially appointed as U.S. ambassador to the United Nations in 2005—controversial, in part, because his track record on the United Nations had been scathingly negative and almost psychotically intemperate.

Some lesser known but important figures have powerful positions as well, such as Paula Dobriansky in the State Department, Peter Rodman in the Department of Defense, and Zalmay Khalilzad, who was White House liaison to the Iraqi opposition before the war and has now been rewarded with the appointment of U.S. ambassador to Iraq. Others have come and gone, such as former Deputy Secretary of State Richard Armitage and Richard Perle, chairman of the advisory Defense Science Board, who resigned from that post after a lobbying scandal and is now quietly plying his trade with the quintessential right-wing think tank, the American Enterprise Institute. PNAC has also mobilized other well-known right-wing figures of varying distinction and talent, such as Jeb Bush, Steve Forbes, Dan Quayle, and James Woolsey, the former CIA director who is probably mostly forgotten except for his ludicrous attempts to link both 9/11 and the anthrax letters in the United States to Saddam Hussein.

The list of PNAC members and signatories overlaps to an extraordinary degree with Anne Norton's list of "Straussians," which I mentioned earlier. While Norton seems to want to distance Strauss himself from his acolytes among the neo-Straussians, there are some intellectual commonalities, particularly in their understanding of politics as a realm characterized by a definitive, almost Manichaean struggle between friend and enemy (a view echoed—or perhaps debased—by George Bush's strong-arm assertion after 9/11 that nations were "either for us or against us" in the struggle against terrorism). That principle warrants the elaboration of a general theory of leadership or statesmanship of the sort that Carnes Lord elaborates in *The Modern Prince:* the ideal leader in a democracy is essentially an authoritarian protector of the people and the people's interests (Abraham Lincoln, Winston Churchill, and Margaret Thatcher are all often cited as instances in this regard). Such a leader would be entitled to act in ways that one might not ordinarily think of as democratic—using secrecy and deception in the interests of the very people who are being deceived and kept ignorant. The leader here is guided by superior political and philosophical wisdom that the many cannot comprehend.

Such a view of the many, the people, implies corollary positions. As Shadia Drury suggests, a neo-Straussian believes that "[m]odernity is the age in which the vulgar many have triumphed. It is the age in which they have come closest to having exactly what their hearts desire— wealth, pleasure, and endless entertainment." In the face of the corrosive effects of modernity's commodified culture, neo-Straussians—in this instance well exemplified by Allan Bloom and his elitist views of culture—would wish for the revivification of older, more serious virtues and social relations, including the revival of the martial virtues.

These "neo-cons are ideologues, not opportunists," then, according to Michael Lind. So while the recommendations of PNAC are essentially about foreign policy and are basically concerned with issues of American power, they are supported by a matrix of ideas that implies a broader neoconservative ideology. The foreign policy ideologies are, as Eric Hobsbawm has pointed out, essentially utopian: they have dreamed up and are in the process of trying to realize "the last of the utopian projects so characteristic of the last century" (*The Guardian,* March 9, 2004). But that very utopianism is built on a more general and idealized notion of America. Thus it is no surprise that, while most of PNAC's members and fellow travelers have taken up one sort of administrative position or other, the organization also has what we might call an ideological arm. That is, a number of its other members have long been prominent voices in the culture at large. Led by Gary Schmitt as executive director, the original PNAC signatories included a whole list of right-wing think-tank hacks, writers, and publicists, none of whom have ever had any difficulty getting their views aired in the U.S. print and electronic media: they include Midge Decter, Francis Fukuyama, Norman Podhoretz, William Kristol (editor of the conservative *Weekly Standard*), Donald Kagan, Fred Ikle, Frank Gaffney, Gary Bauer, and William Bennett.

It has been the task of these public figures to found the offensive foreign policy strategy on what Bennett has called "the dictates of our moral and political traditions." Joined by the usual extremist conservative hit men, like Ben Wattenberg, Charles Krauthammer, and Michael Novak, PNAC's ideological arm was first in line after 9/11 to call for a violent response, while at the same time proposing that such an action would be based in what Robert Kagan called "moral clarity and courage." Such rhetoric appealed not just to a sense of justifiable righteousness in the face of the terrorist attacks, but equally and simultaneously to a sense of America's special moral status, its role in the world as what Kagan had called "the indispensable nation" whose values should be made to be "applicable to all men at all times." From that mixture of idealist notions, a simple formulation to explain the attacks was forged: that what had been attacked was America's exceptional moral status, and the best way to vindicate that status was to attack its enemies. The formulation was further reduced for public consumption: "We love freedom . . . they hate freedom."

Such a fundamentalist appeal to essential American values is evidently part of the construction of a "you," as I have already discussed. But what the values actually are that underpin the appeal is nearly always slightly fuzzy and vague—even if the rhetoric used to propound them is often ruggedly pointed. One book published in the wake of 9/11 and in the run-up to the Iraq war, William Bennett's *Why We Fight: Moral Clarity and the War on Terrorism* (2002), is a particularly good place to locate the underlying values. Bennett predictably argues post–9/11 for a violent response and justifies it by way of arguments against Christian pacifism and by an assault on claims that Islam is a peaceful religion. But the central justification he gives is the simple assertion of a generalized and idealized vision of an America whose tradition is "morally purposive, self-correcting, and glorious" (70). "Ours is, in truth," he proclaims, "a good system, a superior way of life, a beacon and an emblem for others" (48).

A large part of Bennett's book is designed to answer the question of why his own sense of these fundamental American values is not necessarily shared by real Americans, and the largest part of his answer is that American schools, colleges, and universities are teaching something different. Instead of the truth about America's god-given greatness, they teach—and the media and the larger culture amplify the lessons— relativism, nonjudgmentalism, and the insufficiency of truth claims. For Bennett, relativism is the biggest crime, and it is, in and of itself, anti-American: "[A]nti-Americanism . . . is the inevitable consequence of relativist thinking" (66).

It has to be concluded, then, that to be properly American, one must be antirelativist, and the conclusion seems even more warranted after Bennett has several times poured scorn on what he assumes to be a typically relativist, anti-American statement: "[O]ne man's terrorist is another man's freedom fighter." Bennett does not seem to be able to consider that this statement is, in fact, empirically true; for him, it is simply false. The point, however, is that the truth of such a statement entails the beginning of political thought and calculation (what are we to do about the fact that one man's terrorist is another's freedom fighter?). For Bennett, it is not the beginning of politics, but exactly the end. Thus his answer to the question of "why we fight" is that "we" believe a priori in the correctness of "our" perception. The only course left, when faced with a true statement that "we" do not believe, is to short-circuit political and legal processes and exert "our" correctness through violence. Far from exhibiting the moral clarity that it claims for itself and for America, Bennett's thinking is thus in the end an eschewal of political and civic processes and of legalism, every bit as irrational as the taunt from the Vietnam era that it ultimately resembles: America, love it or leave it.

Bennett's particular articulation of the supposed moral basis for American violence is itself a kind of utopian vision, unabashedly deployed in support of the utopian ideal of American hegemony in the world. I take his position as exemplary, but it is far from unique. The past few years have seen a steady rise in the language of American moral superiority, especially in discussions of the Iraq farrago. The ideologues of the right have insisted, for instance, that even the worst excesses and horrors of the invasion and occupation can be defended as morally and ethically superior if compared with those of Saddam Hussein's regime. Christopher Hitchens, once a figure on the left of U.S. public discourse and now exhibiting all the zeal of the converted, has specialized in that sort of proposition, as well as in a more general rejection of anti-Bush positions that depend, in his argument, on assuming a moral equivalency between American and non-American instances of violence and law-breaking. For Hitchens, what the Bush administration has perpetrated in Iraq was morally necessary, and his own supporting discourse drips with moral righteousness: speaking, for example, of a book that he calls "a haunting account of the atmosphere of sheer evil that permeated every crevice of Iraqi life under the old regime," he claims that "it is morally impossible to read it and not rejoice at that system's ignominious and long-overdue removal." For Hitchens, the disastrous and illegal war and occupation are better than having done nothing to counter "Islamo-fascism" and the evil of Saddam Hussein: thus are all kinds of sins of commission and omission waved into insignificance. Like many of his new friends in Bush's camp, Hitchens rarely admits into consideration any of the economic aspects of the current conjuncture. In the contemporary right-wing versions of the world, the economic is at best a technical issue to be submerged beneath a discourse of moral and ethical argument.

One exception to this might appear to be the work of Niall Ferguson, whose book *Colossus: The Price of American Empire* makes a case for the benefits of American imperial ambitions in mostly economic terms. Ferguson tries to show that in the history of colonialism and imperialism "there was such a thing as a liberal imperialism and that on balance it was a good thing" (198). It was good essentially because it brought economic growth and profitability to both the colonizer and the colonized and fostered the supposed benefits of global free trade and technological advancement. Ferguson recommends this kind of liberal imperialism for the current moment; he suggests, for instance, that a country like Liberia today "would benefit immeasurably from something like an American colonial administration" (198). Yet it is hard to escape the conclusion that all Ferguson's argument does is drape new clothes over the familiar suppositions of ideologies of Third World underdevelopment and over the moral justifications for the "civilizing" mission of imperialism. Ferguson is not overtly a member of the "America the virtuous" chorus, but his underlying assumptions certainly could not stand without a thorough confidence in American benevolence and altruism.

Those kinds of assumptions are an essential component, of course, in the neoconservative ideology of American superiority. Claes Ryn has tried to articulate some of what constitutes this ideological basis by deploying the old republican term, *virtue*. Ryn sees the ideological aspect of the current regime as the instantiation of what he calls "a new Jacobin ideology," resting on a sense of the essence of American virtue that is universal in appeal and can and should be applied everywhere. In fact, as Ryn explains at length, this isn't at all a new ideology, but one that has been apparent in U.S. culture at least since Woodrow Wilson (we should say, it has been here for much longer), but he argues that it has steadily gained influence since the Reagan years and has finally reached a hegemonic position since 9/11. Its transmutation from a utopian ideology to an empowered logic of policy has rendered the United States "prejudiced against the traditions of old, historically evolved nations and groups . . . [whose] societies and cultures should yield to the homogeneity of virtuous democracy' (396). Interestingly, Ryn sees George Bush himself less as a chronically convinced ideologue of this neo-Jacobin ideology and more as a recent convert. He points to the change in Bush's position since 9/11; until then, Bush had actually shied away from the project of "spreading freedom and democracy"—a staple of the previous twenty years of policy—and been much more of an isolationist. The events of 9/11 gave the neo-Jacobins the opportunity to push "democratism," as Ryn rather neutrally calls it.

As I've suggested, this virtuous democracy depends on an image of Bennett's "glorious America," and the relationship is reciprocal. In other words, the rhetoric of the virtuous ideal and that of the imperial are bound together, and each justifies the other. What the two notions share, so to speak, is their antirelativism, that component of thinking that rests on a priori certitude. In other words, for these neoconservatives, their belief is a self-authorizing absolute that inevitably warrants the imposition of will. This fundamental sense of correctness—a primitive belief in the all-encompassing power of one's own thinking—is a form of narcissistic disorder (in the sense I have used that term in previous sections), inimical or at least indifferent to the norms of human intercourse like tolerance and empathy, discussion and negotiation, self-restraint and self-questioning. The narcissistic urge then masks its habitual indifference by pronouncing itself the medium of the most elevated ideas and benevolent ideals. Thence the kind of spectacle that Bush presented in his 2005 State of the Union address when, in the midst of the worst moments in the altogether terrible Iraqi war, he elided all problems attendant on his foreign policy and simply urged (fifty-three times) the utopian benefits of the abstraction, "freedom."

## fascism

The relationship between the foreign policy imaginary and the narcissistic sense of America is, as I've said, symbiotic: the one formation enables the other. Thus the logic of the domestic actions of the Bush government have to be seen as inextricably linked to the logic of its foreign policy actions. The post–9/11 domestic happenings are simultaneously a necessary precondition to and a necessary consequence of U.S. attempts to gain hegemony in the interstate system. Just as the peculiar role of the United States in international imperialism is crucial to understanding what is happening inside its borders, the state of America in the age of Homeland Security is crucial to understanding the specificity of current imperialism. However much the present shifts in American culture can be seen as late manifestations of already chronic trends and characteristics in the culture, they seem extraordinary in many ways and to many people—to the point that they are often described as "fascist," or at least as authoritarian. My argument here will be that, however much the current American regime is abhorrent, it seems hardly sensible to dub it fascist. Indeed, to do so is to make a number of analytical and probably strategic errors. Aside from the potential trivializing of historical fascism, perhaps the most egregious error is the misrecognition of the very different relations between labor and capital in historical fascism compared to contemporary America.

Most important, historical fascism has always engaged some kind of mass movement (usually with an active militia) that crosses class lines and indeed could be said to reorganize class formations altogether. This is simply not happening in contemporary America, where it makes more sense to say that one of the crucial goals of current neoconservativism is the continued subjugation of labor and the reinforcement of class formations. Equally, fascism—even in its occasional populist American forms—has always been anticapitalist in ideology, and it should be clear by now that, whatever the populist rhetoric of the current regime, its fundamental interests are with a fundamentalist capitalism. Whereas historical fascist economic systems depended on an ever-increasing corporatist organization of the economy along with thoroughgoing state control, the organization of the contemporary American economy is far more diversified and in many respects beyond the control of the state. And while it is true that the current regime often adopts a negative approach to the constitutional and legal habits of American democracy (as I will discuss later on), it could scarcely be likened in most respects to the twentieth-century regimes whose antagonism to liberal democracy always intended its demise and replacement by a single-party state. And few would argue that Bush (even leaving aside that his terms are constitutionally limited), or probably any other U.S. politician could ever be produced as the charismatic and rallying leader required by historical fascism. And this is to leave aside other characteristics of historical fascism, notably a rallying call for national regeneration, a totalizing concept of politics, and the primacy of politics, all accompanied by stylistic rituals and ideologies.

In those respects, then, to dub contemporary America fascist is not very useful. Indeed, the general description of historical fascism might apply rather more to the displaced regime of Saddam Hussein than to that of the United States. (I have taken many of the elements of my broad description of historical fascism from Stanley Payne's excellent *History of Fascism, 1914–1945* [1995] and I take seriously his remark to that effect.) That's not to say, of course, that the epithet might not have some affective and rhetorical mileage for some in opposing the current administration's policy, but the term risks becoming debased in the same way the term *imperialism* was in the Vietnam years. But perhaps the main problem with the use of the term is the way it deflects attention from the fundamental operations of the United States today at the level of the wage relation. I've already tried to argue for the centrality of the wage relation to the interstate imperial system and thence to the American role in that. The efforts to spread the capitalist form of class relations around the globe are paralleled by intensified efforts to strengthen and deepen them at home. According to Leo Panitch and Sam Gindin, the current phase of those efforts stretches back to the monetarist reforms of the early 1980s (to the very beginnings of the phase that comes to be known as "globalization"). The principal aims of those reforms (and their high interest rates) were "to break the back of inflation and the strength of labour" (60). The ensuing liberation of financial markets is at the root of globalization itself and has led relentlessly to the weakening of labor in relation to capital. A simple demonstration that the process continues can be seen in the Bankruptcy Reform Act, passed by Congress in 2005, which pulls away one of the few protections remaining for the working classes against the effects of rampant liberalization of credit and the massive expansion of financial markets.

So not only would it be historically inaccurate to think of the United States as fascist, but attention is deflected away from the fundamental processes of capital in doing so. Having said that, however, I'd suggest there is indeed an argument to be made that the United States has entered a period that might properly be called authoritarian in a way that is reminiscent of what Hannah Arendt describes in *The Origins of Totalitarianism* (1951). For Arendt, the preconditions for twentieth-century totalitarianism (for her, fascism and communism) arise through authoritarianism, first with the bourgeoisie's abdication of the political process and the concomitant enfranchisement of what she calls "masses," and then with the ensuing breakdown of the class system and proper class representation by political parties. I have just argued that, far from breaking down, the class system in the United States is becoming reinforced, and in that sense current conditions do not conform to the rise of authoritarianism as Arendt sees it. While in the economic sense class formations have become more rigid, in the political sense they have only a fantasmatic appearance. That is, the ideological effort (arguably the same effort as throughout the whole of U.S. history) has been to eradicate class consciousness from the political realm, all the better to control the economic realm and hide its objective operations. In the present moment, the "meaningless politics" of contemporary America has all but severed any remaining link between class consciousness and political representation, such that at the levels of both political and civic life, the kinds of conditions that Arendt points to are replicated.

The displacement of class, or the relation between labor and capital, is facilitated in contemporary America by the extension in the public sphere of what Arendt calls the "rise of demagogues, gullibility, superstition, and brutality" (316). The primitive ideological appeals of right-wing radio shows and evangelical Christianity, on the one side, and ruggedly doctrinaire speech and action by the political class on the other, both heighten the sense of authoritarianism. At the level of state activity, Arendt sees the formation of what she calls an increasingly "anti-utilitarian state" with an "unprecedented concept of power," operating within the cover of an "ideologically fictitious world," and with a rhetoric that is always "millennial" (417). These characteristics have in one way or another been perceptible in American culture in the post-9/11 period; all of them have been at least intensified at the start of the twenty-first century, and they constitute an increasingly secure ideological climate for the imposition of authoritarian practice.

Domestically, the most overt assertions of the authoritarian will have come in the form of the Patriot Act and the steady erosion of civil liberties that has stemmed from that act. (This is to put aside for the moment—until the next section—the exercise of authoritarianism in relation to enemy combatants and prisoners and with regard to human rights.) Many of the effects of the legislation, justified in the name of the war on terror, are well known, even if resistance to them is minimal within the United States. They need little rehearsal: systematically discriminatory legal scrutiny and treatment based on race, national origin, or religion; the criminalization and punishment of speech; secret detentions and extralegal proceedings; apparently unfettered government access to private information and data (on matters such as book buying and borrowing, computer use, and so forth); increased surveillance— governmental and private—across all realms of public activity; government "eavesdropping" on telephone conversations, and so on. These measures have restructured daily life in all kinds of ways: from intensified airport security, new security measures, and an armed presence at almost every public place, to routine phone-tapping and other information-gathering activities, to the appearance of license plates that suggest we "Fight Terrorism." The introduction of the Patriot Act and the formation of the Department of Homeland Security helped imbue the culture of the nation with a continual sense of danger, presided over by increased but increasingly distant governmental urgency and authority.

In a way, it should be no surprise that Americans have given themselves over to such new controls and to the straitening of their much-vaunted liberties. And equally, it should be no surprise that they effectively voted in 2004 to condone and retain this authoritarian formation. The tendency of Americans to first vote for and then submit to what de Tocqueville used to call the "tutelary" power of government has been a chronic one: "They feel the need to be led and they wish to remain free," and they shake off their dependency on the state only long enough to vote it in and then relapse into dependency and apathy once more (664). And just as the urge to military imperialism has cropped up across the whole history of the republic, so, too, has the urge for authoritarianism at home. I would contend, however, that the current moment constitutes a coincidence of the interstate imperial and the domestic authoritarian that is historically unique for this nation.

legal matters

tanley Payne's otherwise instructive and thorough account of historical fascism, from which I have drawn to outline the features of fascism proper, makes little or no mention of fascism's relation to the law and legal structures. This is, however, one aspect of fascist regimes that receives repeated attention in Hannah Arendt's *The Origins of Totalitarianism*. Notably, Arendt argues that the whole arena of the German juridical system (legislatures, courts, coded laws and constitution, and so on) had to be essentially evacuated and reformulated for fascism to take firm hold. She notes, too, that the rise of fascism necessarily included the attempt "to kill off the juridical in man . . . putting certain categories outside the protection of the law, forcing the non-totalitarian world into a recognition of the lawlessness . . . [and setting up] concentration camps outside of the normal penal system and selecting inmates beyond normal procedure" (447).

Arendt's point is readily confirmed in most respects by one of the few works devoted to the Nazi legal system, Ingo Muller's *Hitler's Justice: The Courts of the Third Reich* (1991). The primary goal of Muller's popular book is to show how Nazi jurisprudence was in fact rooted in the prefascist moment of Weimar Germany (and, of course, to demonstrate that strong elements of it survived long past the end of National Socialism). Muller's analysis of the process whereby fascism took control of the law anxiously stresses the fragility of all legal structures when, as with the Nazis, there is some intention to manipulate or refashion the law, not simply ignore it; when, in other words, the strategy is to take control of the legal system in order to allow it to produce a new version of legality. The underbelly to this assault was the claim that the judiciary had become alienated from the people and the people's will. The Nazis complained about the degeneration of law into a merely technical legal procedure in which the idea of "real justice" had been lost, and they engaged in a cultural campaign to denigrate the legal profession (Hitler himself famously declaring that "[t]here is no one to whom the lawyer is closer than to the criminal"). In the years since 9/11, the general themes laid out here have some resonance with what has been happening in America. Beyond the unavoidable issue of detentions in Guantánamo Bay and elsewhere, and beyond the nexus of the Patriot Act, which has had the effect of rearticulating constitutional norms, the general tone of American views toward the judiciary suggests a clear authoritarian trajectory.

In some ways eccentric to this process, but in others ways extraor-
dinarily illuminating, is the much-publicized Terri Schiavo case in 2005,
in which the Congress, with President Bush's support, passed an emergency law to help ensure the extension of Schiavo's life in a persistent
vegetative state. The ideological effort of this law—to endorse in a
spectacular way the so-called "culture of life"—was perhaps less egregious than the simple fact of its passage. It has long been a tenet of U.S.
constitutional law that laws cannot be written arbitrarily and opportunistically for specific individual cases, and jurisprudential deference
to individual states' versions of due process has been consistent since
the 1884 *Hurtado v. California* case. The Schiavo law, in demanding a
de novo review by federal courts of state process, was a brazen abnegation of these constitutional norms and it flew directly in the face of the
opinion in *Hurtado:*

> Law is something more than mere will exerted as an act
> of power. It must be not a special rule for a particular
> person or a particular case. . . . Arbitrary power, enforcing
> its edicts to the injury of the persons and property of its
> subjects, is not law, whether manifested as the decree of a
> personal monarch or of an impersonal multitude. . . . The
> enforcement of these limitations by judicial process is
> the device of self-governing communities to protect the
> rights of individuals and minorities, as well against the
> power of numbers, as against the violence of public agents
> transcending the limits of lawful authority, even when
> acting in the name and wielding the force of the
> government. (110 U.S. 516, 535–36)

Without such enforcement, the opinion suggests, "a government . . .
which [holds] the lives, the liberty, and the property of its citizens subject at all times to the absolute disposition and unlimited control of even
the most democratic depository of power, is after all but a despotism."

The willingness—nay, the eagerness—of the U.S. Congress and the
president to break long precedent to pass a law (as Florida governor
Jeb Bush had also tried to do previously in this case) that essentially

pertains to one person and one case only is what is most striking here, and most unsettling. This manipulation of the law was, I would claim, enabled and even emboldened by a longstanding right-wing campaign against contemporary legal practice, lawyers, and judges and the supposed perversion of the law by special ideological interests. That is, the complaint uttered by Schiavo's father during his efforts to keep her alive echoes a sentiment that has become almost a mantra in contemporary America: that "the judges are running this country." And that view has consistently been expressed as a complaint that judges and the courts are "activist," using rulings from the bench to shape political policy.

Carnes Lord concisely and conveniently sums up the various elements of this general antagonism in his book, *The Modern Prince*. Among his many other complaints, Lord damns the current courts for their susceptibility to "ideological pleading" from feminists, environmentalists, and assorted unsavory fellow travelers. According to Lord, even those most disreputable discourses, "social science methodologies . . . and postmodern literary theories have been plumbed" for anything that could fund the perversion of legal opinion making (131). Lord also repeats the oft-made assertion that justice is being perverted by "litigious trial lawyers" (132), a claim urgently expressed by right wingers who scarcely bother to hide the fact that it is made in favor of corporate and state powers over and against the interests of the individual citizen. Lord's work is an example of the neo-Straussian ideology that begins with the idea that politics as such is a discrete field that can and should be isolated from other areas of civic life, like the law. This positivist theorem has been elevated to the status of an article of faith for today's neoconservatives and perhaps has no more overt an application than in their view of the law. The supposed politicization of law is more than just a technical offense in which the law has been perverted or diverted by special interests and greedy lawyers. Rather, it is an almost ontological offense because one component of civic life has been allowed to contaminate another.

So according to Terri Schiavo's father and his allies among the neoconservative intellectuals and politicians, the judges are running this country. And in a certain sense, they are right. At a moment when political processes are indeterminate and many civic and cultural issues are logjammed in some way (everything from abortion to presidential elections themselves), the legal system is frequently called on to resolve these issues in unprecedented ways. In other words, where the state and the mainstream media have produced politics that are "meaningless politics," it inevitably falls to the judicial system, as the only open channel, to take on the task of trying to resolve issues in the relationship between citizen and state. But this *should* be one of the roles of the law and generations of legal scholars have recognized it as such: the law is inescapably a political function of the state, and its characteristics change with the contingency of history. The neoconservatives who deny this purport to be able to separate the realm of the political from the processes of civic life. Not only is this a factitious separation, but it is also, contradictorily, a quintessentially political claim—and one that has immediate political effects.

Some of those effects are, of course, simply discursive, such as Mark Levin's demotic, indeed, rabble-rousing book, *Men in Black—How the Supreme Court Is Destroying America* (2004), in which Levin complains of a "de facto judicial tyranny" in America and calls for the active removal of "radicals in robes" who make law rather than interpret it. Levin's ideological home is perhaps revealed by the book's front and back matter—written by Edwin Meese and Rush Limbaugh. Listeners to the latter's radio show and indeed to Levin's own radio contributions will be familiar with the upshot of these clarion calls—the expressed desire to remove activist judges, by force if necessary. And indeed, the right-wing antagonism has led to acts of violence against judges: the 2005 murder of a state judge in Atlanta and the 2005 slayings of a federal district court judge's husband and mother in Chicago, not to mention chronic assaults on abortion clinics and on lawyers and judges seen to be pro-choice. Even where such acts of violence seem topically motivated, their possibility has been chronically prepared for and enabled by the repetition of the charge of judicial activism, which is made everywhere from Bush's campaign speeches and congressional confirmation hearings to radio talk shows. Texas senator John Cornyn made a notable splash in the aftermath of the Schiavo case by appearing to endorse violent acts against judges who "are making political decisions yet are unaccountable to the public" (*Washington Post,* April 5, 2005). (One of the most rabid primitivists in Congress, the unspeakable Cornyn was at the time speaking in defense of the indefensible—the application of the death penalty to minors.)

Much of the activism and rhetoric of this antiactivist campaign depends on—and, I would argue, ultimately derives from—a quite problematic and historically compromised understanding of the law. That is, it depends on notions similar to those deployed in Nazi Germany to advance the rise of authoritarian power. At the center of such notions is the proposition of some kind of *natural* justice that stands above and beyond instantiated or institutionalized legality. For the Nazis, existing law had become divorced from natural law and natural justice, in part because of the technical overcomplexity of a legal system that rendered, in the notorious Nazi phrase, "justice divided from the people."

The National Socialist idea of natural justice made a link, in ways that are historically familiar, between the delivery of "real" justice and the establishment of mystical concepts of the nation, national community, the national soul and history, and so on. And certainly it is the case that the antilegalism of the Nazis was one of their weapons in a more total effort to dismantle Germany's liberal constitutional state. In those respects, the experience of Germany is quite specifically fascist. Yet the idea of a natural justice that could and should always trump existing institutional law was fundamental to the process of establishing an authoritarian state and it has its own expression in America—not just among today's right-wingers, but also in the history and mythographies of the American republic. They sit, for example, behind the most popular fictions of the frontier and behind the primitive ideology of vigilantism. In other modes, they appear as appeals to some sort of religious or mystical "higher power," a God capable of delivering proper or final justice where the law itself is seen as somehow not sufficiently effective or just.

Once again, Carnes Lord provides the exemplary formulation of this legal fundamentalism when he suggests that "the common law has been increasingly eclipsed as a source of legal judgment, and with it a way of thinking that is not embarrassed to understand law as an *inherently reasonable* enterprise that is *grounded in the nature of things*" (131, my

emphases). I tend to think that one *ought* to be "embarrassed" to imagine that there is any form of rationality at all that corresponds to some
natural order, but it seems clear in any case that this is what Marx might
have recognized as a weird sort of physiocratic illusion; at the very
least, it is an unproven article of faith that bespeaks a certain kind of
primitive and even theistic view of the natural world.

Such appeals to natural law, or to a higher form of justice that
trumps institutional law, have, of course, been particularly strident in
the aftermath of 9/11. The invasions of Afghanistan and Iraq were both
predicated on a rejection of existing legal options, including the rejection of existing criminal law as incapable of delivering justice in the
wake of the terrorist attacks. William Bennett disputes the claim that
terrorists should be sought by police action rather than military action,
suggesting that "by appealing to courts and lawbooks, and especially
under the cloak of 'international' jurisdiction . . . matters of fundamental right and wrong were once again being elided" (33–34). Somehow the available systems of law would not be able to account for the
particular atrocity of 9/11, which in fact would only be "trivialized,"
according to Bennett, by being treated under existing law.

The multiple ways in which the Bush administration has followed
the basic logic of Bennett's argument will be news to no one, and so I
will not enumerate them here; but it is worth pointing out that the
logic is applied now not only to international issues, but to domestic
ones as well. The scandal that erupted over domestic wiretapping early
in 2006 is a good example of how the administration appeals to this
particular aspect of its legal posture. The idea is that the peculiar circumstances after 9/11 demonstrated the incapacity and inefficacy of
existing legal structures, including those laws passed by Congress. As
far as those latter laws are concerned, the Bush administration consistently proposes (as I will discuss below) that the constitutional power
vested in the president allows (indeed, demands) that he should be free
to execute them only within the limits of his own interpretation of the
Constitution. Thus, in the domestic arena, individual rights are threatened not by their complete or sudden excision, but as in the case of
Nazi Germany, by their being overshadowed or squeezed out by rights
that are held by the state or, in this case, by the president alone.

The wiretapping issue, of course, is just one of the many that have demonstrated how vexed, not to put too fine a point on it, the current administration's relation to the law really is. In relation to international, constitutional, criminal, and civil law, there has been a clear and consistent pattern of assertion that existing legal standards and practices are inadequate, and not just for waging the "war on terror." The Bush government exhibits a generalized disdain for international law, treaties, and international obligations (such as the Geneva Conventions and the International Criminal Court), much as it does for the "litigious lawyers" and "activists in robes" that it discovers at home.

But the clear project in all areas having to do with the law has been not so much to disobey or ignore the law as to remake it, and there is, it seems to me, a central notion that ties the various efforts together. This is something that has no analogy in the rise of historical fascism, but is a development specific to the history of the United States and to the peculiar disposition (i.e., separation) of state powers envisaged in the Constitution. That is, Bush and his acolytes have continuously promoted the idea of the "unitary executive" over the last few years, and there is plenty of evidence to say that the administration acts as if the idea were, so to speak, unimpeachable. The notion is derived from the Madisonian idea of a "departmental" government wherein not only are different powers (executive, legislative, judicial) separated, but the judgment of what is and is not constitutional is a task given to all three branches. The proponents of the unitary executive thus claim that Article II of the Constitution gives the power to execute federal law to the president alone, but he is impelled by the duty of upholding the Constitution.

A key figure in articulating this theory appears to have been David Addington, Vice President Cheney's legal counsel, whose daily work reportedly involves ensuring no encroachment on presidential power and privilege. Addington was the author of the notorious "torture memo," a proud achievement, but in other issues he has had no qualms about arguing for the need to withhold information from Congress and the public, or the need to remove supposed terrorists from juridical reach. His exposition and implementation of the unitary executive idea is perhaps the single most important theoretical and ideological motor of the current regime's actions. It has, predictably, also been one of the least discussed, though it did appear as a matter of concern for senators in the 2006 nomination hearings for Supreme Court Justice Samuel Alito. There the attention was, however, desultory and almost directly a result of senators' concern about Alito's membership in the Federalist Society—a powerful group of right-wing lawyers founded in the 1980s that includes many members who have served under Ronald Reagan and/or one or both of the Bush presidents. Both Alito and President Bush's other recent Supreme Court appointee, John Roberts, have been deeply associated with the group (even if Roberts, in a Peter-like denial before his nomination vote, claimed to be unable to remember his membership). The idea of the unitary executive is, as far as I can discern, the invention of the members of the Federalist Society and their cadres in the Reagan administration, including controversial legal scholar John Yoo.

The aim of the unitary executive theory is ultimately not just to protect the prerogatives of the president's power, but to render the executive branch the preeminent of the three branches of government, and it is this aim that most reveals the incipiently authoritarian nature of this project. Various devotees of the theory have been quite open about the aims here, including Dick Cheney, who has suggested (much to the disbelief of most legal scholars) that over the past few decades, the presidency has been enfeebled to the degree that presidents cannot do their job properly. The authoritarian urge here should not be under-estimated, of course, but for Bush himself, the "unitary executive" seems to be understood as the equivalent of "strong leadership"—at least, that is the sound-bite version of it that is deployed in his speeches. But of course the significant upshot of the idea is more extensive than the relatively benign call for strength in leadership, and the nature of the upshot can be glimpsed by examining some of the devices that Bush consistently uses to instantiate the "unitary executive."

Among those devices is the presidential signing statement. In his first term alone, Bush wrote over four hundred of these statements, which are appended to acts of Congress upon their signing. In most instances, Bush's statements question the constitutionality of the act, frequently pointing out encroachments on presidential prerogative. In most cases they affirm the president's right to interpret the new law according to his own understanding of the Constitution. That is, Bush's regular comment on duly established laws is to express his right to reinterpret them. In that sense, a signing statement often has the effect of a quiet veto (and their frequent use might go a long way toward explaining why Bush does not use direct vetoes). Perhaps the most public instance of this is the statement Bush added to the 2005 McCain bill banning the use of torture: there Bush reserves the right to issue orders for torture at the very moment that he signs the antitorture bill into law (and even as he makes his famous announcement to the media and the public that "we do not torture").

Akin to, and perhaps even more important than, these signing statements are executive orders and letters. It is worth remembering that some of the chronically controversial and divisive domestic issues brought up during Bush's two terms arise from executive orders he has issued—faith-based initiatives, for instance, or limited federal funding for embryonic stem-cell research, not to mention his early antiunion executive order allowing federal employees to reduce their union payments if they do not agree with union policy and action. Equally, executive orders have been used to neutralize the antiballistic missile treaty with Russia and to withdraw the United States from the Kyoto agreements on carbon emissions. And in 2003, in Executive Order 13292, Bush signed over to the vice presidency intelligence powers that arguably exceed the constitutionally established role of that office and certainly give Cheney an amplified role in intelligence and foreign policy.

Even beyond the particular actions perpetrated by Bush through these instruments, the genius of the "unitary executive" thinking is that it manages to say that even the actions most likely to be thought of as unconstitutional are in fact justified by the most central element of the president's oath of office, namely his promise to protect and execute the Constitution. The constitution becomes a kind of extralegal fetish or totem: it stands as the mark of a higher power in relation to the everyday legislative process of the republic, and yet it is still not properly interpreted, so it becomes the president's job to do so. In this regard, there's perhaps little need to recall the analogous appeal that Bush famously makes to higher authority, nor to recall his much-remarked tendency to believe himself the chosen agent of such a higher authority. (In a different book, much could no doubt be made of the psychoanalytical component to this faith.) Suffice it to say that the Constitution, as understood by Bush and his acolytes, stands in relation to the law as sacred scriptures do to a religion. The fundamentalism of Bush's supposed personal faith is thus mirrored in this factitious view of the Constitution: that the president's constitutional powers allow him to interpret the Constitution to say that he is not breaking the law, even as he is breaking it.

It goes without saying that the current administration's posture in this regard, handily summed up in the phrase "unitary executive," has been permanently at play in the post–9/11 moment and culminates in the breathtaking ambit of presidental power that the administration claims as a result of Congress's authorization to use force in the "war on terror." Bush's stated understanding of that authorization and its relation to the power of the unitary president is that it is essentially a carte blanche. Certainly in the media-induced "scandal" over the use of domestic wiretapping early in 2006, the administration's argument leaned heavily on that congressional authorization.

But the same underlying reasoning—namely, that the president is constitutionally empowered to execute the law according to his own interpretation of the Constitution—crops up all across the post–9/11 landscape. Arguably, this reasoning lies behind the determination to maintain and defend some of the most controversial—not to say, sickening—aspects of the "war on terror," namely, torture, extraordinary renditions, and the continued operation of the detention center at Guantánamo Bay. But whatever its effects and whatever it is used to warrant, the reasoning is on its face circular and self-serving. It constitutes a logical sleight of hand pulled off by neoconservatives such as Yoo, Addington, and Lord. What it serves ultimately is the establishment of, if not exactly a Nixon-style imperial presidency, more of an authoritarian regime under the protective cloak of the Constitution. And in its very irrationality, it elevates the Constitution to the role of a fetish, to be interpreted by the presidential shaman.

*animals*

The establishment of such a totemic view of the Constitution, atavistic as its ideological motives may be, clearly amounts to a particular kind of *politicization*. It is, indeed, the prerequisite fundament for the "political *religion* of constitutionalism" that Carnes Lord has called for (230). But, as Marx argued in regard to the various post-Enlightenment constitutions in Europe and America, their primary aim is to establish and protect the power of the political state, while simultaneously producing a "universal secular contradiction between the political state and civil society" (Marx and Engels, *Collected Works* 3: 159). The human or civil rights that these constitutions dispense thus have the limited function of guaranteeing the self-interested, monadic nature of subjects (citizens) within the structure of that "universal" contradiction. Ultimately, in other words, constitutional rights both strengthen the political state and insulate it from the contradiction it creates with civil society. This is achieved in part by legislating for a particular kind of subject:

> None of the supposed rights of man . . . go beyond the
> egoistic man, man as he is, as a member of civil society,
> withdrawn into himself, wholly preoccupied with his
> private interest and acting in accordance with his private
> caprice. (164)

This "man," roughly equivalent to what I have called the subject of value, is the subject to whom rights are eventually restricted and around whom the carapace of political state power can be built. As Marx proposes, "it is man as a bourgeois and not man as a citizen [i.e., as a member of civil society] that is considered the *true* and *authentic* man" (164). Beyond such a *political* subject, the subject of civil society is seen as necessarily nonpolitical and indeed as some sort of "natural" man for whom political rights could never be germane. In other words, the constitutional discourses of the post-Enlightenment reserve a whole area of human subjectivity to the *extra-political,* and thereby construe a nonpolitical subject that is by definition beyond the ambit of rights.

The Bush administration's atavistic view of the U.S. Constitution reads this split between the political and the civic to the letter. Or rather, their extremist view has the aim and effect of refreshing that distinction and exacerbating a contradiction that has been chronically endemic to American life and culture. I have already pointed out how this dichotomy is played out in a quotidian way in the confusion of notions of equality and freedom—the one being a political attribute of the subject of value and the other being merely its inflected symptom, rather than the political right that it is so often taken to be. For now, I want to stress how such a view opens the way to delimiting or curtailing political rights in the name of the "natural"—that is, the nonpolitical. I would argue that the division of the political from the civic, of the arena of political rights from natural rights, is what warrants and authorizes the kinds of civil rights and human rights abuses that this administration has routinely engaged in. At the very least, it makes clear the logic whereby certain subjects in certain circumstances can be denied access to rights.

The Long War has generated many such instances, both domestic and international, where this view of the subject combines with the posture in relation to the law that I described above to justify the abrogation of civil and human rights by the U.S. administration. The examples hardly need to be enumerated at this point, but obviously the penumbra of this mode of thinking covers Abu Ghraib, Guantánamo Bay, "black sites," and extraordinary renditions. Equally, it covers the government's attempts to ignore the conventions of habeas corpus in a number of terrorist cases, like that of José Padilla; or to reduce the ambit of rights legislation, as in the case of Zacarias Moussaoui; or to brush aside domestic constitutional rights by wiretapping domestic phone communications. All these highly publicized instances are perhaps just the tip of the iceberg. They depend, at least, on a logic that is theoretically extensible such that (a) the requisite defining characteristics of the subject of value might be met by fewer and fewer subjects, and (b) the circumstances under which the political can claim isolated autonomy from the civic might become more narrowly defined. It would perhaps not be stretching a point to suggest that the victims of Hurricane Katrina, for example, have learned something about the first of these conditions, or that the Long War has proved useful in facilitating the second of them.

In particular, the Long War has facilitated the effective ostracism of whole classes of people from the realm of "appropriate" subjectivity. Such people are, of course, "the enemy," as Bush likes to dub them—the jihadists, combatants, and fellow travelers whose status has been decided *in advance* of any political and legal proceedings. The "enemy," in this view, has always already been stripped of all rights and can be treated, eventually, as little more than an animal. This reduction to the status of animal warrants and encourages the kind of unsophisticated treatment that the United States has notoriously been doling out. This animalistic enemy is the subject of the detention center in Guantánamo Bay, and of the prison at Abu Ghraib, and of extraordinary renditions, of course. The extralegal status preassigned to them ensures that, once captured, they can be subjected to whatever forms of treatment the U.S. government feels are appropriate, whether it be torture as such, physical and mental abuse, terror tactics, force-feeding, or cultural and religious humiliation. The point is perhaps illuminated at the very moment in September 2006 when the Bush administration moved a number of prisoners from the hitherto unacknowledged CIA "black sites" to the detention center in Guantánamo. Their removal was loudly accompanied by the claim that they were finally going to be brought to trial. That claim not only drew unwelcome attention to the fact that these prisoners had spent years in legal limbo, but also underscored the even more uncomfortable fact that they still had no agreed legal status. The U.S. Supreme Court in the summer of 2006 had already declared the planned military commissions for Guantánamo prisoners to be unconstitutional, and no other legal mechanism had yet been put into place.

The United States has made it clear at the legal level that these subjects are not worthy of or appropriate for the legal protections of either constitutional or international law. They are simply "evil," literally outlaws. They need not, therefore, be seen as common criminals, or even ultimately as individuals. As Dick Cheney pronounced, they "don't deserve to be treated as criminals. They don't deserve to be treated as a prisoner of war. They don't deserve the same guarantees and safeguards that would be used for an American citizen going through the normal judicial process" *(New York Times,* November 15, 2001).

These subjects, removed from the political and legal realm, are effectively thrown back to some putative "natural" state where their supposedly inherent "evil" is their only quality. These are people who, in Arendt's terms, have been rendered "the savage, animalistic other, not properly endowed with humanity but only human animality" (301). That is how Arendt describes the status of the Jews at the hands of the Nazi state. Giorgio Agamben describes it similarly, as the reduction of the human being to the *zoe,* the animal. Agamben further claims that this creature can be dubbed the *homo sacer*—in Roman history, the holy sacrificial subject that can be exterminated by sovereign power without guilt or remorse. For Agamben, the *homo sacer* is the privileged figure of the meeting place between politics and power and the existence of life itself, and that represents the inclusion within the realm of politics of what politics in fact excludes—what Marx might have recognized as "species being." The figure of the *homo sacer* is in that sense a deconstructive commutational device by which Agamben wishes to mark the uneasy boundaries between the realms of the political and the civic.

The notion, however, that the subject legally and politically reduced in this way to an animalistic status is somehow held as a ritualized and sacralized subject seems to me a dubious conclusion in the current conjuncture—or indeed within the specific history of America altogether. That is, throughout the history of the republic, the proper place of the outlaw, precisely, has been the civic realm, where the correct mode of dealing with that figure has been the principle of revenge and punishment meted out by civil society. One of the specific ideological features of American life has chronically been the application of extralegal sanctions in the civic realm, and in a sense the boundaries between the civic and the political have been consistently solid in a way that Agamben's schema would not be able to recognize. This all takes place in the arena of the "natural"—where the "natural" nonpolitical outlaw subject is confronted by the principles of "natural" law and justice. In the imaginary of American "natural" justice, the human animal is punished, rather than sacralized, and the executioner is not the sovereign or the state, but the populace.

Agamben's notion of the *homo sacer* does, nonetheless, capture something of what is happening here in the throes of the contradiction between political and civic life, but his schema is generally quite metaphysical and ahistorical. Most notably, Agamben would seem ill-equipped to account for what I am suggesting is happening right now, post–9/11: namely, the wholesale importation of the tradition of "natural" justice into the political realm precisely to allow for the exaction of punishment and revenge. That is to say, the *homo sacer* of the present moment can no longer be described as the liminal or commutational figure that marks the porous boundary between the political and the civic. The *homo sacer* has perhaps turned into a figure like Zacarias Moussaoui, the subject of demotic revenge and punishment. The post–9/11 scenario is such that there can now be an absolute coincidence between the *political* trial of the supposed "twentieth hijacker" and the demotic urge for revenge that was perhaps most visible during his trial in the shape of the relatives of 9/11 victims regularly expressing for the television cameras their eagerness for a death sentence.

Moussaoui, the captured al-Qaida enemy subjected to revenge and punishment, barely escaped the absolute reduction to the animalistic that marks the fate of other representatives of "the enemy." And the detainees at Guantánamo Bay and Abu Ghraib have experienced the material effects of what it means to become the extralegal human animal. At the level of representation, at least, the archenemy Osama bin Laden also has been reduced to savage animality, represented in American public discourse as groveling around in the primitive caves of a primitive landscape. The same kind of attempt to show the enemy as animalistic was perhaps even better served by the circumstances of the capture of Saddam Hussein. Few will forget the discovery in 2004 of the subhuman Saddam, captured in his so-called spider hole, where he had been reduced to the most basic functions of life before being paraded like a dog before the world. The conduct of his American captors immediately afterward produced some of the most remarkable images of the Long War: the CNN video and its still outtakes of Hussein being examined by American doctors. Hussein's treatment brought a strong rebuke—one of many outside America—from a top Vatican cardinal, who condemned the public humiliation of "this man destroyed, [the military] looking at his teeth as if he were a beast." The images were indeed chilling. The medical technician, looking like some doctor from a sci-fi movie inspecting an alien, shines a light into the animal's throat, set against what is almost the anthropometric grid of the imperial anthropologist. The examination echoes the inspection of slaves at a market, Jews in a prison camp, or horses at a sale, and thus marks the complete mastery over this dangerous yet humiliated animal.

The dissemination of the media images of Saddam was clearly a deliberate strategy on the part of the administration and the U.S. military—and no doubt contravened the Geneva Conventions' injunction against public humiliation of prisoners of war. But especially at a time when the Bush administration had already sidelined the Geneva Conventions, very little was ever going to be said, or be allowed to be said, in the culture at large questioning or objecting to the treatment itself, still less the "mere" depiction of that treatment. Indeed, the CNN video and its stills, beamed across America and immediately flooding the Internet, by and large met with the requisite barbaric response. The BBC Web site featured an image of two American fans at a football game, beers in hand, their chests naked, brandishing a homemade banner: "We Got Saddam." Their victorious barbarism was only enhanced by the fact that they had painted their torsos red for their team, the Kansas City Chiefs, one of several NFL teams that persist in the exploitation of Native American signifiers.

The subsequent trial of Saddam Hussein has, of course, returned him to human status. The same transformation is effected on the CIA prisoners who were transported from CIA "black sites" to Guantánamo in 2006—their animal status, deriving from "natural" law, is revoked as soon as codified law is invoked and the extralegal subject has to be pulled back to the political realm. But the politico-legal structures prepared for both Saddam Hussein and the CIA prisoners remain at best shaky. The Bush administration transported the CIA prisoners to Guantánamo in preparation for trial even though no approved constitutional mechanism yet existed for such trials, and Saddam Hussein had been handed over to a hastily concocted Iraqi court that he had every reason to describe as a tool of the American occupiers. In both cases, for these humans returned from the status of animals, the likely outcome is the death penalty. Hussein's trial is, as most commentators have seen, a farcical affair. It would not even have taken place under the auspices of Iraqi sovereignty were it not for the fact that the Iraqi court, with all of its legal authority and process having been dictated under the imprimatur of the U.S. occupiers, would permit the death penalty. That most primitive form of human punishment is one thing that the cultures of the United States and its Muslim allies and foes alike understand and appear to accept, and their sharing of this outrage to humanity will forever alienate them in their barbarism from the rest of the world.

## human rights

*I* have been suggesting that the promotion of a primitive belief in some sense of natural law—based, as Lord puts it, in "the nature of things"—has facilitated the establishment of an at least inchoate authoritarian politics in America. The fact of 9/11 has made this all the more possible, but it is a feature of American culture and life that has been always ready to be activated, as it were. From the historical problem of vigilantism, to the widespread claims for "victims' rights" and objections to the Miranda laws, through to the Patriot Act today, American culture is replete with instances of a chronic struggle with (and an attempt to assimilate) a primitive logic holding that established law is too technical and sophisticated to produce "real" justice.

This logic finds an interesting echo in Jacques Derrida's discussion of the law. Derrida's essay "The Force of Law: The 'Mystical Foundation of Authority'" draws a broad ontological distinction between Law and Justice, and claims that the Law as a system is never *juste* (never exact) because such a generalized system cannot account for and respect the particularity of an individual case. As distinct from a Kantian form of determinate judgment, which established law is, Derrida wants to champion instead what he calls individual "acts of justice"; these, he says, "must always concern singularity, individuals, irreplaceable groups and lives, the other or myself as other." He claims further that "if I were content to apply a rule, without a spirit of justice and without in some way inventing the rule and the example for each case, I might be protected by the law . . . but I would not be just" (17). The point here is that, from the vantage of the logic of deconstruction, no system of established law has solid grounds for authentic authorization and universal application. Whatever the lure of such a logic (and it should be admitted that there's good reason to wish that the law could indeed encompass all singular cases), the danger is the alternative that Derrida chooses: to protect particularity and singularity, he appeals instead (by way of Kierkegaard and Levinas) to some mystical or primitive foundation for legal authority.

The issue here in the end is that deconstruction, relying on the principle of undecidability, on the irreducible claim to the otherness of the other, cannot condone the Law because there is no determinate ground by and through which it might legitimate itself. (It's interesting to note, as an aside, that before and after the invasion of Iraq, Derrida seems to make a different kind of appeal. With Jürgen Habermas, he writes two "open letters" that call for some kind of constitutionally based supranational legal order that would have the ability to forfend the American actions.) This deconstructive view of the Law is, in the end, not so different from the Bush administration's view of what counts in the Long War. Domestic and constitutional law and established rights, international law and treaties like the Geneva Conventions, international criminal proceedings, and courts of law are apparently not appropriate for the terrorists in the view of the Bush administration and many in Congress, not to mention the media. In the wake of the supposedly extraordinary crime of 9/11, real justice can apparently be delivered only beyond the law, and the most immediate upshot of such a conviction is the suspension or distortion of constitutional rights.

As Agamben has amply demonstrated in his *State of Exception* (2005), the suspension of rights under the guise of preserving them is nothing new; indeed, it has become a common practice of government. In the

course of his discussion of how emergency situations ("states of exception") are called on to provide cover for an authoritarian abnegation
of constitutions and rights, Agamben deals at length, of course, with
the process whereby the Nazis undertook this course. But he also notes
some specifically American instances, from Lincoln's Civil War suspension of habeas corpus, to Woodrow Wilson's and Franklin Roosevelt's
claims to special presidential powers in states of emergency (claimed by
Wilson during World War I, and by Roosevelt to wage a "war" against
the forces of the Great Depression). These instances are often invoked
in the current moment to justify the Bush administration's activity in
the Long War that has now been declared. The kinds of powers claimed
are dependent on the definition of a state of emergency as a war. Thus,
Agamben says,

> President Bush's decision to refer to himself constantly
> as the Commander in Chief of the Army after September
> 11, 2001, must be considered in the context of this
> presidential claim to sovereign powers in emergency
> situations. If as we have seen, the assumption of this title
> entails a direct reference to the state of exception, then
> Bush is attempting to produce a situation in which the
> emergency becomes the rule, and the very distinction
> between peace and war (and between foreign and civil war)
> becomes impossible. (22)

It's perhaps worth digressing here to point out how Britain's Tony
Blair, America's only important ally in the invasion of Iraq, shoulders
the whole weight of this kind of authoritarian move when he baldly
claims that his government's controversial antiterrorism bills, constantly
in evolution since 9/11, are "not destroying our liberties, but protecting
them" (*The Observer,* February 26, 2006). Over the past few years Blair
has pledged himself to a series of draconian detention laws and to
various other measures that clearly help erode civil liberties in Britain,
all in the name of the supposed state of emergency or exception: "If the
nature of the threat changes," he claims, "so should our policies." His
path of action flies in the face of a 2004 ruling by the British House

of Lords, which rejected some of the proposed laws on the indefinite detention of terrorists and was clear about the basic democratic issues at stake. While recognizing the theoretical right of the executive to define states of emergency, the ruling made it clear that the "war on terrorism" was definitively *not* such an emergency as to put the life of the nation at risk, and it was equally clear about the invalidity of the British executive's revocation of habeas corpus.

If Blair's position echoes the rhetoric of the Bush administration in many respects, there is a crucial difference: namely, Blair's refusal to fall back on a discourse of "natural" justice to subvent his claims and policies. In the American context right now, such a recourse is, on the contrary, crucial to the project of rolling back constitutional rights. But equally, as I have discussed, the current administration has added the device of the "unitary executive," so that the pursuit of "natural" justice can be conducted under the aegis of that peculiar constitutional theory. On one level, the application of this double movement would seem to confirm Agamben's notion of the "state of exception" by showing how the state of emergency or war can become permanent. On another level, there is something very specific to the American context about this simultaneous appeal to both a civic principle ("natural" law) and a political (constitutional) principle. That is to say, even if Agamben seems correct when he suggests that the state of exception has become somehow generic, the norm for the exercise of sovereignty, this is a generalization; the specificity of the American situation has been prepared for and enabled by the peculiar history and structure of the republic.

Under an ideology of "natural" law, any "determinate" system of law can be held to be insufficient under multiple circumstances. Thus, this opportunistic ideology can be stretched willy-nilly to underpin an assault on any kind of legality. In the current moment, its powers are also increased by way of the religious component that suggests that, if the law is not just, then there is a higher justice. But of course it is clear that such an ideology of the law is itself founded on nothing much more than irrational conviction posing as absolute principle, a fundamentally *mystical* authority. By contrast, it would seem important right now to insist on the principle that justice cannot be founded on some notion of an irretrievable natural order of things, but must always call on a contingent foundation, based in the changing sociocultural understandings of the people who are subject to the law.

The attraction of the natural law thesis, however, has been increased precisely by the state of emergency that the political state has called into place. Certainly, the claim appears to be easier to make at a point when terrorism has been named the enemy and has been made to appear as an immediate threat to the sovereignty of the republic. It is a combination of this appeal to a natural justice and a simultaneous view of terrorism as a threat to sovereignty that permits the political state to regard its perpetrators as beyond both law and morality—and, increasingly, as beyond the canons of human rights.

The importance of the question of human rights has increased tremendously over the past decade or two in the interstate system; indeed, it has become one of the crucial components of international relations under the aegis of the United Nations and has been impelled by the acceptance of strong human rights standards in the European Union in particular. The United States is often credited (and often credits itself) with being a leader in the formation of this burgeoning human rights regime, and no doubt there is some merit to that view. On closer inspection, however, the posture of the United States toward human rights is exceptionally ambivalent. And this ambivalence has become all the more evident since 9/11 and the declaration of the Long War. The current American rhetoric is that it is the war on terror and indeed the terrorists themselves that have provided ample justification for the application of rules and policies beyond the conventional: terrorists constitute the state of exception. The reality is that the United States has de facto made itself an exception in the realm of human rights by using the Long War to justify serious abnegations of what had been a growing international consensus on human rights standards and protocols.

Of course, there is a need to be wary of the whole regime of human rights, even beyond current American diffidence. As John Milbank correctly observes, there is a clear "racist basis" to the history of human rights discourse and practice: "This 'universal' notion was originally invoked by the West in order to intervene in the internal affairs of non-white countries," to be sure (311). The vulnerability of human rights discourse, and a point of controversy as far back as Burke's critique of the French Revolution, has always been in the claim to universalism. That is, in proclaiming the possibility of a determinate system of human rights based on the idea of a common *humanity,* the discourse of rights comes immediately up against essentially *political* questions of application, access, enforcement, and remedies. In other words, and in light of what I have suggested earlier, the gap—or the contradiction—between political subjects and human subjects becomes visible and germane at the very point that human rights can be invoked at all. Something of what this entails and the consequences of this gap are clear in America after 9/11. As Milbank suggests, as soon as the security and sovereignty of the North is threatened by terrorism, the immediate response—the necessary consequence, in fact—is an abnegation of human rights: "[I]t becomes clear that rights are things that archetypically belong to 'American citizens' under 'normal,' which means local and not at all universal, circumstances" (312).

The prospect of the United States retreating from the principles of universal human rights has had many obvious features, a number of which have already been mentioned here. The consequences of the American posture can perhaps be fairly illustrated by the fact that anyone so far released from Guantánamo Bay has been rescued only by exceptional negotiation with other nation-states, and not by any autonomous preference on the part of the U.S. government. Even though the Supreme Court in 2004 weighed in on behalf of detainees who are national subjects and in 2006 declared administration plans for military trials unconstitutional, no one has yet been released either by dint of being found innocent in any legal process or as the result of any appeal to their human rights. The five hundred or so detainees remaining in Guantánamo can essentially be regarded as *political prisoners* and therefore, by definition, *not* the subjects of human rights. These detainees have not simply been consigned, as Arendt said of the Jews in Nazi concentration camps, to the "merely human"; they have become political prisoners who are "civically dead" (300).

Arendt herself actually takes a Burkean view on universal human rights: that is, she adopts the position that generalized human rights are of little use under the conditions where they would need to be invoked, since those conditions always already include the debasement of the human subject to the condition of the "merely human," and indeed, to the condition of the animal. The Burkean response to the European ideal of universal human rights was always that such rights can make sense only in a national context where the subject is a political citizen rather than a human subject. The stark difference between revolutionary European universalism—or its new EU and UN forms—and the kind of Burkean conservativism espoused by the United States right now was exposed in the Supreme Court's ruling in the summer of 2004: American citizens were given protection from the Bush administration's policy of indefinite detention, but noncitizens—specifically the so-called "illegal combatants"—were left with no protection. Many of them remain, treated like animals in Guantánamo Bay or in various U.S.-sponsored prisons and torture chambers around the world.

The problems with the current American human rights agenda and with the Burkean hand that the United States is playing go far beyond the treatment of specific subjects by the United States. If there was any clear planning for the aftermath of the post–9/11 military adventures in Afghanistan and Iraq, it was that sovereign states were to be (re-)established there. Thus, at the level of rights, there would be no regime of rights possible before the full functioning of sovereign states. An often overlooked or unmentioned element of the Abu Ghraib prisoner abuse scandal—not to mention the abysmal human rights record of the United States in Iraq more generally—is exactly that it was enabled by the fact that it took place in this lacuna between two political states. In that hiatus, the United States made no attempt to establish any political rights and also considered itself exempt from international rights obligations. Iraqis, in other words, were deliberately deprived of access to any rights regime between the beginning of the occupation and the passing of a (rudimentary) constitution. The irony, of course, is that at the same time the Iraqis were disenfranchised in this way, American justifications for the invasion were beginning to feature the claim that it was undertaken to secure Iraqi rights and freedom. Meanwhile, having shown itself, in this and many other instances, perfectly content to contravene the principles of universal rights, the United States continually inflicts damage wherever it can on the institutionalization of human rights around the world.

There is, in other words, no current genuine commitment to the principle of *universal* human rights on the part of the United States. The determinate judgments of generalized notions of rights cannot, it seems, satisfy the exception that the United States has constituted itself to be in the international arena. The United States did nothing to allay continued suspicions about its human rights agenda on the occasion of the establishment of a new human rights commission by the United Nations in March 2006. The United States was one of only four nations to vote against the new agreement, its official position being that its provisions were not strong enough to prevent nations with negative human rights records from being part of the new commission. But it's hard to push aside the suspicion that the negative vote of the United States was provoked, not just by Ambassador Bolton's customary loutishness, but by the fear that under the new rights regime, the United States would be required to be open to monitoring of its own human rights record, just as much as, say, China.

The final judgment on America's human rights posture might in fact be best left to China—counterintuitive as that might seem at first blush. Not many would want to claim that China is itself a paragon of human rights practice (though some might give credit to its own claims that it is steadily evolving toward international standards). But criticism of China can by no means invalidate the contents of the official Chinese response to the 2006 U.S. State Department human rights report, which accused China of a variety of human rights violations. The Chinese response, provided in a document titled "The Human Rights Record of the United States in 2005," takes a correctly broad view of what might constitute human rights, painting a depressing picture of contemporary America that might be salutary to summarize here.

Taking first the cherished American rights to "life, liberty and the pursuit of happiness," the Chinese response summarizes the violence and danger (murder, violent crimes, the threat from elevated gun ownership—in short, what Baudrillard in *America* has called "autistic and reactionary violence" [45])—experienced every day in America. That violence is linked to the massively compromised state of economic, social, and cultural rights in the United States. The features of endemic social inequality, as documented by the Chinese, include extensive homelessness and hunger in the American population, lack of access to health care for millions, spotty labor and safety rights, and so on. These everyday inequalities and abuses are also marked by the scandalous racial divisions of the United States, as well as by gender and the situation of children. The document points to the vast numbers of American children brought up in poverty, as well as the fact that American culture criminalizes children in ways—and numbers—that few other nations would tolerate. The total number of minors, for example, sentenced to death in the United States in 2004 (sixty-three) was matched by no other country in the world.

These multiple infringements on human rights occur in a culture that is heavily, and not always legally, policed. The report enumerates a whole range of official malfeasance by law enforcement, judicial organs, and the state: from the government eavesdropping scandal to the Patriot Act, from racial and ethnic profiling to police abuse and wrongful convictions. These official actions are set in the context of a nation with one of the largest prison populations in the world, and with regular reports of mistreatment in prisons, as well as illegal detentions and searches on an everyday basis. And even at the level of political rights and freedom, the Chinese indict the United States for its dubious election processes and the financial brokering of not just elections themselves, but the actions of the representatives elected.

Only after this lengthy catalog does the report cite the overt human rights violations of the Long War. In contravention of America's own laws and treaty obligations, as well as in violation of international law, the well-known violations at Abu Ghraib and Guantánamo stand alongside the use of secret prisons, extraordinary renditions, the widespread use of torture, and inhumane and degrading treatment. But perhaps even these outrages pale in comparison to the deaths and injuries that the United States continues to inflict on civilians, not just in Iraq and Afghanistan, but wherever it feels it is necessary. The Chinese report concludes simply: "The facts listed above show the poor human rights record of the United States, which forms not only a sharp contrast with its image of a self-claimed 'advocate of human rights,' but also a disaccord with its level of economic and social development and its international status."

As far as I'm aware, the United States has never officially responded to the Chinese indictment. If it were to, one might easily imagine that justifications of the most overt or publicized human rights abuses would come in the shape of appeals to the "state of exception," to the security demands of the Long War—and would perhaps do little more than confirm Marx's charge that "security is the highest social concept of civil society, the concept of *police*, expressing the fact that the whole of society exists only in order to guarantee to each of its members the preservation of his person, his rights, and his property" (Marx and Engels, *Collected Works* 3: 163). Or else, an American response might predictably question the way the report conflates human rights with civil rights. But what the Chinese document makes clear is exactly the necessary connection between human and civil rights, as well as the indefeasible relation between the most spectacular U.S. abuses (those of the Long War) and the everyday conditions of this republic—conditions that are the simple corollary of America's primitive devotion to its particular form of capitalism. Ever since de Tocqueville took it as given that Americans enjoyed "equality of condition," American freedoms have been confused with the notion of equality. But the Chinese document also highlights the fact that freedom is by no means the same as equality, and the confusion of the two leads to (in fact, dare I say, *constitutes*) the abuse of human rights. In primitive America, in other words, rights are not rights to equality; at best they are just delimited political rights to freedom. And to insist again on some of Marx's words, in this context even freedom "is not the freedom of one individual in relation to another, but the freedom of capital" (*Poverty of Philosophy*, 207).

## precarious politics

At the very start of this book I affirmed that this was not to be yet another assault on the Bush administration (though the specificity of the post–9/11 situation amply warrants such assaults), and that my own emphasis was to be different. I hope, since then, to have laid out as simply as possible a sense that America did not change on 9/11—at least not in the ways that "you" are assured. What has happened, rather, is that many of the basic constitutive features and historical tendencies of the American republic and its history have emerged into configurations that perhaps seem new, but cannot be said to be unprecedented or alien to the culture. What I have been calling "the primitive" is a set of formations and tendencies that have long been present within the history and culture of America, but that have become more prominent in the past few years and have inflected anew the dialectic between the "hot" and the "cold" elements of American life.

At the same time, it is obviously true that the American reaction to the events of 9/11 has been spectacularly shocking and has inevitably produced all kinds of resistance and opposition, both at home and abroad. I want to turn my attention for a moment to a particular voice of American critique that I believe is emblematic of the kind of oppositional utterance that is common right now. As the post–9/11 wave of hysteria and narcissistic agitation has abated somewhat and as the Iraqi war has come to seem daily less justifiable, public and intellectual discourses have begun to admit the critique of numerous aspects of the administration's conduct. Judith Butler's book, *Precarious Life: The Power and Mourning of Violence* (2004) is one such critique, and I want to examine it here, not just because Butler is generally understood to be a doyenne of radicalism on college campuses across the country, but because her work demonstrates both the attractions and the limitations of what I see as a merely liberal critique.

*Precarious Life* is a series of essays in which Butler addresses the post–9/11 scenario by critiquing the exclusionary, media-led response to 9/11 and America's lack of a moral sense of the lives of others (notably Muslims). She addresses at length the outrage of Guantánamo Bay and the Bush policy of indefinite detention, and objects to the unevenness of the discourse that the Israeli-Palestinian conflict is accorded in U.S. public life. The book's final essay is a rather straightforward discussion of the philosopher Emmanuel Levinas framed in an argument about the role of criticism in these times.

Given that Butler frequently stresses the poverty of media-led public discourse, it should be pointed out that since the appearance of her book, the tide of American media discourse has been turning. Since roughly the beginning of 2004, many parts of the media—led, perhaps, by *The New York Times* and CNN—have been visibly releasing themselves from the onus of their self-defined duty to slavishly reproduce the most impoverished of all possible American responses to 9/11 and its aftermath, which the Bush administration had manufactured for them. The media's change of tone had begun before the infamous pictures from the Abu Ghraib prison, but it was solidified by them and then fueled by a whole series of events and revelations: America's practice of extraordinary rendition, allegations about secret prisons and torture, the Valerie Plame affair and the indictment of Scooter Libby, and governmental eavesdropping or "Snoopgate," among others. A real tipping point, arguably, was Hurricane Katrina and the application of the administration's heady mix of incompetence, callousness, and dishonesty to the suffering caused by America's biggest natural catastrophe. Certainly that event precipitated an abysmal drop in Bush's poll numbers and warranted continuing media pressure on the administration.

The mainstream media are still "embedded" in all kinds of ways to be sure; but from the position of being pigheadedly in the tank for the Bush administration, they have been slowly recovering the ability to critique the whole post–9/11 farrago both at home and abroad, the misadventures in Iraq, and Bush himself. There are, that is to say, positions and arguments now disseminated that, pace Butler's numerous asides about the poverty of contemporary conditions of representation, provide the elements of opposition. It's no longer just some maverick, unpatriotic liberals complaining, for example, about the Patriot Act and the general assault on civil liberties, about Rumsfeld's barbaric policies in Guantánamo Bay and Abu Ghraib, about civilian casualties in Iraq, and so on. These are positions that many on the political spectrum have now taken, continue to take, and presumably will have to keep on taking. Indeed, in the past few years people like Jonathan Schell from *The Nation* and Sidney Blumenthal from *Salon.com* have tirelessly made the same essential arguments that Butler does in her book—but in venues and language that are more widely accessible. Many of her points have been more concisely made in national newspaper editorials (and some of them were even made by John Kerry on his notoriously nonantagonistic campaign trail). And this is not to mention the appearance of a series of remarkable political documentaries, like *The Control Room, Outfoxed, Bush's Brain,* and Michael Moore's *Fahrenheit 911,* or cable television programming, which regularly airs assaults from the likes of Jon Stewart and Bill Maher. In the publishing world, hundreds of books have appeared critiquing all different aspects of the post–9/11 mess, from Noam Chomsky's *9/11* and books by authors like Robert Bahr, Chalmers Johnson, and Lawrence Wilkerson, to the now-renegade neoconservative Frances Fukuyama and his *America at the Crossroads* (2006). None of this is to say that the air of impunity around the administration does not remain, but it is to assert that critique is rampant and thus it is just as hard to credit Butler's positions with any originality as it is to disagree with them.

But the point I want to make here is that the body of analysis and criticism of which Butler's book is a part joins the lists mostly at the level of moral, ethical, and political debate. That is, making connections between the political-economic posture of this nation and the current scenarios does not appear to be a priority for most commentators. Some, like Chomsky, will of course point to the general conditions of worldwide capitalism as the direct cause of an American imperialism, while others, like Johnson in his *Sorrows of Empire* (2004) will point to particular economic factors like the role of the military-industrial complex. But it's fair to say that most critiques that gain any prominence in public debate foreclose on discussion of the general conditions of capitalist America. To be sure, there is always some discussion about the role of oil, and there is also the affectively gratifying prospect of Michael Moore's economic conspiracy theories, but by and large, mainstream public discourse and analysis are confined to the moral and political dimensions of the current situation, while the political-economic remains generally that which cannot be said.

The same is essentially true of Butler's work. She ties her book together by way of themes and propositions that are familiar from her previous work—notably the notions of human "relationality" and subjective "identity"—and those themes are deployed exclusively within an ontological and ethical framework. That is, Butler's most insistent argument is that normative notions of what constitutes "the human" have to be rethought and reformulated. A central instance of what I'm pointing to comes early in the book, when she proposes to consider "the conditions under which certain human lives are more vulnerable than others, and thus certain human lives more grievable than others" (30). She asks why, for instance, Americans cannot grieve the Muslim dead in the post–9/11 conflicts. But the absence of the Muslim dead from the news and the obituaries is immediately aligned with the struggles of "sexual minorities . . . transgendered people . . . intersexed people . . . [the] physically challenged" and racial minorities, all of whom struggle with the social imposition of parameters of the human, with normative values and "culturally viable notions of the human." This sweeping homology is driven home by reference to "the queer lives that vanished on September 11," who apparently went unrecognized in the obituaries and whose relatives were only "belatedly and selectively . . . made eligible for benefits" (35).

This rather breathtaking alignment has perhaps the opposite effect to that intended. Here and elsewhere, Butler is at pains to say that she's not calling for simply some warm and fuzzy inclusion of the excluded subjective into the faulty normative schemes that she sees all around her. Instead, she is calling for what she calls "an insurrection at the level of ontology" (33). If that's to be the new slogan of radicalism, Bush, Rumsfeld, and their ilk probably aren't going to lose a lot of sleep. But this rather fatuous phrase does at least have the merit of prompting the question of what Butler's revolution would have to consist in, or what kind of subject would have to be mobilized. But rather than offering ways to reconceive interrelational subjectivity, or even simply highlighting the specific struggles of different subjects, Butler in effect produces nothing more than some rough equivalency among all those who somehow don't currently fit neatly into the "culturally viable notions of the human" (33). To conceive of such an equivalency, one has to do a lot of stripping away of materiality and be virtually impervious to questions of specificity.

At best, what Butler is pointing to here is a purely discursive or ideological homology, and it turns out to be a very incomplete homology, even in its own terms. That is, there's something analytically wrong when Butler's highlighting of the "lives vanished" from the World Trade

Center cannot include the laborers, janitors, food workers, homeless people, and undocumented immigrants who died or suffered, and whose struggles for recognition were not just about their access to "culturally viable notions of humanity," but equally about their economic value. That is, in largely unpublicized struggles to gain compensation and benefits, the relatives of many of these people, as well as attack survivors themselves, have confronted the simple fact that those lives were simply *not valued*. The struggles of many of these people who fail to reach the definition of the subject of value continue, years after the attacks.

These kinds of people don't appear in Butler's pantheon of victims—and her chosen victims themselves do not appear as labor, nor as subjects whose identity is in any way constituted by their relation to capitalism (even though this might well be why they were attacked, as putative representatives of a predatory capitalist expansionism). This elision is more than simply symptomatic of Butler's approach—an approach that is essentially a plea for freedom and equality in a context where, as I've been suggesting in this book, freedom and equality are each other's neutralizing masks). The elision is, rather, a reminder of the weakness of any consideration of subjective identity that cannot or will not entertain the historical and material conditions under which such identities are formed.

In the end, what divides and differentiates subjects is not some factitious, contingent, and unsatisfactory use or application of the category of the human. Rather, it is the continual and relentless depredations of capital. So it's not really *conditions* that Butler investigates in her work. She isn't asking about American imperialism, or media power, or any of the material factors that inflect contemporary ideologies. And she is certainly not talking about any *material* form of subjectivity. Rather, she is simply pointing to some of the discursive structures and attitudinal habits that are devolved symptoms of those conditions.

Butler herself would no doubt be familiar with the criticism that she is unable or unwilling to investigate material conditions or see subjects as produced by them in any significant way. Similar issues are notably at stake in her well-known exchanges with figures such as Nancy Fraser and Gayle Rubin in the past decade; they arise again in her conversations with Laclau and Zizek in *Contingency, Hegemony, Universality* (2000). In my view, Butler comes across in these exchanges as more obstinate than correct when dealing with the challenge that politico-economic factors pose to her thinking. Indeed, in the last named text, when called to account for these lapses, she comes out with one of the most perverse formulations in all of her writing: "It's unclear that the subject is not, for instance, from the start structured by certain general features of capitalism, or that capitalism does not produce certain quandaries for the unconscious and, indeed, for the psychic subject more generally" (277). Such circumphrasis (a spectacular double negative and a vagueness masquerading through the repeated word *certain*) can only confirm the suspicion that if an examination of "conditions" entails thinking in terms of political economy, Butler doesn't want anything to do with it.

The limitations of that reluctance are in full view all across *Precarious Life,* but perhaps nowhere so overtly as in Butler's repeated insistence that the media are to blame for the parlous state of "contemporary conditions of representation" (16). While that may well be the case in some limited sense, the assertion should surely mark the beginning of an investigation, rather than establish the media as a kind of untranscendable horizon; but this underlying assumption about the conditions of representation is never granted explication or elaboration. It seems to me that, even in Butler's own terms, little progress could be made in the "revolution at the level of ontology" without at the same time rethinking those conditions of representation and the role of the capitalist media in enforcing them. Indeed, to reformulate her own words: it is in fact perfectly clear that the conditions of representation are from the start structured by very specific historical features of capitalism.

Butler's way of circumnavigating the material emerges in many other places in these essays. For example, in her chapter on the policy of indefinite detention, she spends several pages explaining Foucault's distinction between governmentality and sovereignty (tapping into a debate that takes many forms and different vocabularies in different disciplines and discourses—though you wouldn't know that from her account). Essentially, she tries to establish a kind of dialectical description of the Bush administration's actions: increases in the bureaucratic processes of governmentality give rise to gestures of authoritarian sovereignty, and sovereignty thence gives itself back over to the mechanisms of governmentality to secure itself. There might be simpler ways to describe the rise of authoritarianism in the post–9/11 administration, and certainly there are alternative ways to describe the same thing. But Butler's chosen mode sets the tone and intent, which is in the end to disembody the political processes involved. Its relation to subjectivity, to the civil being of the subject is absent. That is—and even despite her naming of names (Rumsfeld and Ashcroft in particular)—those processes come to seem unmotivated, untouched by human hand, but also to have no relation to the subject. It's almost as if the administration's sovereign behavior can have no material explanation: it's simply what's happening and its monstrous agents are simply ciphers. Butler's thinking, especially on political issues, often seems to operate in a similar fashion, such that materiality is invoked but evacuated in the same gesture, and where cultural and social processes are regarded more as a structural machine than as motivated forms and processes.

There is, of course, a perfectly standard name for this kind of thinking: this is essentially good old American liberalism. The first two major casualties in that American liberal tradition have always been political economy and history—these factors disappear even as they are ritually invoked in some polite way. A second traditional characteristic is what might be called a creeping universalism, where the very fact of speaking from within the American context soon persuades the speaker that there is a "we" out there that shares our assumptions and perceptions. This is the underlying narcissistic reflex of the American subject that I have discussed before.

A third characteristic of American liberal discourse is its strain of religiosity. Butler's final chapter in *Precarious Life* concentrates on Emmanuel Levinas and it exhibits that trait. The essay is intended to underline the philosophical basis of the book's general discussion of the human and it is, in fact, from Levinas that Butler gets her title. For Levinas, the word *précaire* fully implicates its etymology in the Latin word *precari,* an interestingly intransitive verb meaning to pray. The suggestion in Levinas is that the Other is finally the divinity to whom we must pray and upon whom our existence depends in a supplicatory way. Butler's text doesn't explicitly take on this thicker meaning of *precarious,* but the pressure that the word exerts on her text produces a glimpse of the religiosity that lurks behind all her schemas of interrelational identity.

Like many other instances of liberal oppositional discourses right now, Butler's work has power and it uses that power to identify and assault some of the worst symptoms of post–9/11 America. The liberal's tone is certainly outraged and militant; but it would be a mistake, I think, to take it as radical opposition. Rather, the discourse of the *bien pensant* liberal acts, and has always acted, as the *loyal* opposition, pressing for the right to dissent and question, but never finally questioning or dissenting from the very system that has produced both it and its master. Indeed, the condition of liberalism could be the dictionary definition of precariousness itself: utterly dependent on the system and its rules, always in a supplicatory or petitioning relation to it, wanting to have its voice heard, but certainly never willing to overthrow it. Liberalism is, in that sense, not unlike the "embedded" journalists working hand in hand with the military in Iraq.

All of which brings up the question that Butler's final chapter opens and closes with: what is the role and the use of cultural criticism in these times? Butler's answer is both modest and sententious. What is needed, she claims, is to ensure that dissenting voices are heard within American democracy; those voices will bring "us" back to find "the human where we do not expect to find it, in its frailty and at the limits of its capacity to make sense" (151). In my view, it is crucial to recognize this strain of "cultural criticism" as limited and delimited, whether in its academic mode, where the theoretical underpinnings are open for inspection, or in other kinds of public discourse, where the same collapsing back into moral and ethical positions is simply a given. It is, of course, necessary to attack the same targets the liberal attacks—one cannot *not* attack those targets. But to do so is not in and of itself radical; it is rather the embracing of a definitively *precarious politics,* engaging with the political state, but not with the material conditions of its existence.

It is my contention that much of what passes for oppositional discourse in America is essentially liberal in the ways that I've said Butler's "cultural criticism" is. Indeed, much cultural criticism, in my view, disables itself from the start by refusing to recognize or by simply mistaking the politico-economic coordinates that inflect the very nature of cultural formations. Culture becomes, in much contemporary work, an arena discrete from politico-economic determinations and is thence often posited as in some way or other the realm of subjective freedom and resistance. Such a concept of the cultural reproduces, of course, the idealist division between the political and the civic. But more, this genre of thinking has the effect of distancing or displacing the material question of inequality onto the cultural realm and away from any politico-economic considerations. The extreme endpoint of such a theoretical strategy is the idea of culture as a relatively autonomous arena structured by its own laws, which are not only not inflected by material forces, but actually obstruct or inhibit the logic of the mode of production.

This posture, or some variation of it, is so common on the intellectual left that it has become a shibboleth. I would be the last to dismiss the idea of (or refuse to support the practice of) what might be called cultural contestation, but one of the principal burdens of this book has been to deny the relative autonomy of the cultural and to resist the conflation of the concepts of freedom and equality. Rather, I've wanted to sketch out an image of American culture that takes seriously the fundamental structuring of that culture—with all of its reigning ideologies and mythographies—in its primitive devotion to the processes of capital.

# acknowledgments

*M*uch of the writing of this book was completed while I was on leave from George Mason University in spring 2005 and was a research fellow at the Center for the Humanities at Wesleyan University. I owe the director of the center, Henry Abelove, a great deal of thanks for his welcoming me there, and I hope that I contributed as much to that semester's life at the center as I got back from it. I want to thank Ethan Kleinberg and Quentin Beresford for what I learned from them, and Brenda Keating and Susan Ferris for all their help and friendship. Khachig Tololyan and Betsy Traube, also at Wesleyan University, offered once again their reliable intellectual and personal sustenance.

Many people have helped, supported, and contributed to this project in a variety of ways. I'm particularly grateful to my dear friend Itty Abraham for his eagerness to share and discuss every kind of idea, and for giving me an energizing push at just the right moment. For supportive and critical readings, I'm extremely grateful to Dick Ohmann, Jamie Owen Daniel, John Michael, and Richard Dienst. None of the flaws in the finished product can be laid at their doors, since they each only helped me improve the work. For sundry suggestions along the way (whether witting or not), I thank Sean Andrews, Caroline Bassett, Jean-Paul Dumont, John Eperjesi, Johannes Fabian, Leslie Hill, Larry Levine, Peter Mandaville, George Marcus, Matt Ruben, Tim Shorrock, Elayne Tobyn, and Chris Turner. Pia Moller gave crucial help in the final stages.

My long-suffering editor at the University of Minnesota Press, Richard Morrison, has earned many times over a special word of praise and thanks.

As often happens, the need to speak in public about some of my ideas made for decisive moments in the development of those ideas. So, for such opportunities I thank Laura Mamo and the faculty and graduate students in sociology at the University of Maryland; Johanna Bockman at Global Affairs at George Mason University; and Ananth Aiyer, for inviting me to speak at a forum of the American Anthropological Association.

I owe a considerable debt to the students in the superb cultural studies doctoral program at George Mason University, to many of the program's fellow travelers, and to our fine office manager, Michelle Carr. My special gratitude goes to my closest colleagues and friends in the program: Denise Albanese, Dina Copelman, and Roger Lancaster.

Most important, nothing is possible without my wife, Lisa Breglia, who has changed my life and made it much less cold than I had ever dared hope.

# works cited

Achcar, Gilbert. *The Clash of Barbarisms: September 11 and the Making of the New World Order.* New York: Monthly Review Press, 2002.

Adorno, Theodor. "Sociology and Psychology." *New Left Review* 47 (1968): 79–97.

Agamben, Giorgio. *Homo Sacer: Sovereign Power and Bare Life.* Stanford: Stanford University Press, 1998.

———. *State of Exception.* Chicago: University of Chicago Press, 2005.

Aglietta, Michel. *A Theory of Capitalist Regulation.* London: Verso, 2000.

Ali, Tariq. "Re-Colonizing Iraq." *New Left Review* 21 (2003): 5–19.

Amin, Samir. "Capitalism, Imperialism, Globalization." In *The Political Economy of Imperialism: Critical Appraisals,* edited by Ronald H. Chilcote, 157–67. Lanham, Md.: Rowman and Littlefield, 2000.

Arendt, Hannah. *The Origins of Totalitarianism.* New York: Harcourt, 1968. Originally published in 1951 by Harcourt, Brace.

Baran, Paul. *The Political Economy of Growth.* New York: Monthly Review Press, 1957.

Baudrillard, Jean. *America.* London: Verso, 1988.

———. *The Spirit of Terrorism.* London: Verso, 2002.

Beard, Charles. *An Economic Interpretation of the Constitution.* New York: Macmillan, 1935.

Bennett, William. *Why We Fight: Moral Clarity and the War on Terrorism.* New York: Doubleday, 2002.

Brewer, Anthony. *Marxist Theories of Imperialism: A Critical Survey.* London: Routledge, 1989.

Bromley, Simon. "Reflections on *Empire,* Imperialism, and United States Hegemony." *Historical Materialism* 11, no. 3 (2003): 17–68.

Butler, Judith. *Precarious Life: The Power and Mourning of Violence.* London: Verso, 2004.

Butler, Judith, Ernesto Laclau, and Slavoj Zizek. *Contingency, Hegemony, Universality: Contemporary Dialogues on the Left.* London: Verso, 2000.

Chomsky, Noam. *9-11.* New York: Seven Stories Press, 2001.

Damisch, Hubert. *Skyline: The Narcissistic City.* Stanford: Stanford University Press, 2001.

de Certeau, Michel. *The Practice of Everyday Life.* Berkeley and Los Angeles: University of California Press, 1984.

———. "Walking in the City." In *The Practice of Everyday Life,* Berkeley and Los Angeles: University of California Press, 1984.

Denning, Michael. *Culture in the Age of Three Worlds.* London: Verso, 2004.

Derrida, Jacques. "The Force of Law: The 'Mystical Foundation of Authority.'" In *Deconstruction and the Possibility of Justice,* edited by David Gray Carlson, Drucilla Cornell, and Michel Rosenfeld, 3–67. New York: Routledge, 1992.

de Tocqueville, Alexis. *Democracy in America.* Chicago: University of Chicago Press, 2000. First published in 1835 by Saunders and Otley.

Devji, Faisal. *Landscapes of the Jihad: Militancy, Morality, Modernity.* Ithaca, N.Y.: Cornell University Press, 2005.

Di Leonardo, Micaela. *Exotics at Home: Anthropologies, Others, American Modernity.* Chicago: University of Chicago Press, 1998.

Drury, Shadia. "Noble Lies and Perpetual War: Leo Strauss, the Neocons, and Iraq." Interview by Danny Postel, October 16, 2003. Available at http://www.opendemocracy.net/debates/article-3-77-1542.jsp.

Evans-Pritchard, E. E. *Theories of Primitive Religion.* New York: Oxford University Press, 1965.

Fabian, Johannes. *Time and the Other: How Anthropology Makes Its Object.* New York: Columbia University Press, 1983.

Federici, Silvia. *Caliban and the Witch.* Brooklyn, N.Y.: Autonomedia, 2004.

Ferguson, Niall. *Colossus: The Price of American Empire.* New York: Penguin Press, 2004.

Fromm, Erich. *Escape from Freedom.* New York: Rinehart, 1941.

———. "Politics and Psychoanalysis." In *Critical Theory and Society: A Reader,* edited by Douglas MacKay Kellner and Stephen Eric Bronner, 213–18. New York: Routledge, 1989.

Fukuyama, Frances. *America at the Crossroads: Democracy, Power, and the Neocon-servative Legacy.* New Haven: Yale University Press, 2006.

Gramsci, Antonio. *The Antonio Gramsci Reader.* New York: New York University Press, 2000.

———. *Selections from Political Writings, 1921–1926.* Minneapolis: University of Minnesota Press, 1990.

Hardt, Michael, and Antonio Negri. *Empire.* Cambridge: Harvard University Press, 2000.

———. *Multitude: War and Democracy in the Age of Empire.* New York: Penguin, 2004.

Harvey, David. "Cracks in the Edifice of the Empire State." In *After the World Trade Center: Rethinking New York City,* edited by Michael Sorkin and Sharon Zukin, 57–68. New York: Routledge, 2002.

———. *The New Imperialism.* Oxford: Oxford University Press, 2003.

Healy, David. *U.S. Expansionism: The Imperialist Urge in the 1890s.* Madison: University of Wisconsin Press, 1990.

Hitchens, Christopher. "The Buried Truth," October 8, 2004. Available at www.slate.com.

Homans, George. *The Human Group.* New York: Harcourt Brace, 1950.

Howard, Michael C., and John E. King. "Whatever Happened to Imperialism?" In *The Political Economy of Imperialism,* edited by Ronald H. Chilcote, 19–40. Lanham, Md.: Rowman and Littlefield, 2000.

Huizinga, Johan. *America.* New York: Harper and Row, 1972.

*Hurtado v. California.* 110 U.S. 516 (1884).

Johnson, Chalmers. *Blowback: The Costs and Consequences of American Empire.* New York: Henry Holt, 2000.

———. *The Sorrows of Empire.* New York: Henry Holt, 2004.

Kagan, Robert. "We Must Fight This War." *Washington Post,* September 12, 2001.

Lasch, Christopher. *The Culture of Narcissism: American Life in an Age of Dimin-ishing Expectations.* New York: Norton, 1991. Originally published in 1978 by Norton.

Lenin, Vladimir Ilyich. *Essential Works of Lenin.* New York: Dover, 1987.

Lessing, Doris. Untitled article. *Granta* 77 (Spring 2002): 53–54.

Levin, Mark R. *Men in Black: How the Supreme Court Is Destroying America.* Washington, D.C.: Regnery, 2005.

Lévi-Strauss, Claude. *Tristes Tropiques.* New York: Atheneum, 1972.

Lévy-Bruhl, Lucien. *Primitive Mentality.* New York: The MacMillan Company, 1923.

———. *The Soul of the Primitive.* New York: The MacMillan Company, 1928.

Lind, Michael. "The Weird Men behind Bush's War." *New Statesman,* April 7, 2003, 10–13.

Lord, Carnes. *The Modern Prince: What Leaders Need to Know Now.* New Haven: Yale University Press, 2003.

Luxemburg, Rosa. *The Accumulation of Capital.* New York: Routledge, 2003.

Magdoff, Harry. *The Age of Imperialism.* New York: Monthly Review Press, 1969.

Marcuse, Herbert. *Negations: Essays in Critical Theory.* London: Free Association Books, 1988.

Marx, Karl. *Capital, Volume 1.* New York: International Publishers, 1947.

———. "Economic and Philosophic Manuscripts of 1844." In Karl Marx and Friedrich Engels, *Collected Works* 3: 229–346. New York: International Publishers, 1975.

———. *Grundrisse.* London: Penguin, 1973.

———. "On the Jewish Question." In Karl Marx and Friedrich Engels, *Collected Works* 3: 146–74. New York: International Publishers, 1975.

———. *The Poverty of Philosophy.* New York: International Publishers, n.d.

Marx, Karl, and Friedrich Engels. *Collected Works,* vol. 3. New York: International Publishers, 1975.

———. *The German Ideology.* New York: International Publishers, 1966.

McClintock, Anne. *Imperial Leather: Race, Gender, and Sexuality in the Colonial Contest.* New York: Routledge, 1995.

McIntyre, Richard. "Columbus, Paradise, and the Theory of Capitalist Development." In *Marxism in the Postmodern Age: Confronting the New World Order,* edited by Antonio Callari, 448–58. New York: Guilford, 1995.

Milbank, John. "Sovereignty, Empire, Capital, and Terror." *South Atlantic Quarterly* 101, no. 2 (2002): 305–23.

Montagu, Ashley. *The Concept of the Primitive.* New York: Free Press, 1968.

Muller, Ingo. *Hitler's Justice: The Courts of the Third Reich.* Cambridge: Harvard University Press, 1991.

Nederveen Pieterse, Jan. *Globalization or Empire?* London: Routledge, 2004.

Norton, Anne. *Leo Strauss and the Politics of American Empire.* New Haven: Yale University Press, 2004.

Panitch, Leo, and Sam Ginden. "Finance and American Empire." In *The Empire Reloaded: Socialist Register 2005,* edited by Leo Panitch and Colin Leys, 46–81.

Payne, Stanley. *The History of Fascism, 1914–1945.* Madison: University of Wisconsin Press, 1995.

People's Republic of China, Information Office of the State Council. "The Human Rights Record of the United States in 2005." Released March 9, 2006. Available at the China View Web site, http://news.xinhuanet.com/english/2006-03/09/content_4279287.htm.

Perelman, Michael. *The Invention of Capitalism: Classical Political Economy and the Secret History of Primitive Accumulation.* Durham, N.C.: Duke University Press, 2000.

Project for the New American Century (PNAC) Web site. Available at http://newamericancentury.org.

Rajagopal, Arvind. "Living in a State of Emergency." *Television and New Media* 3, no. 2 (2002): 173–76.

Read, Jason. *The Micro-Politics of Capital: Marx and the Prehistory of the Present.* Albany: SUNY Press, 2003.

Retort. *Afflicted Powers: Capital and Spectacle in a New Age of War.* London: Verso, 2005.

Robins, Kevin. "What in the World's Going On?" In *Production of Culture/Cultures of Production,* edited by Paul Du Gay, 11–67. London: Sage, 1997.

Ryn, Claes. "The Ideology of American Empire." *Orbis* 47, no. 3 (2003): 383–97.

Sardar, Ziauddin, and Merryl Wyn Davies. *Why Do People Hate America?* London: Icon Books, 2002.

Smith, Paul. *Discerning the Subject.* Minneapolis: University of Minnesota Press, 1988.

——. *Millennial Dreams: Contemporary Culture and Capital in the North.* London: Verso, 1997.

Touraine, Alain. "Meaningless Politics." *Constellations* 10 (2003): 298–311.

U.S. Department of Defense. *Quadrennial Defense Review Report.* February 3, 2006. Available at http://www.defenselink.mil/qdr.

Wallerstein, Immanuel. "America and the World: The Twin Towers as Metaphor." Charles R. Lawrence II Memorial Lecture, Brooklyn College, December 5, 2001. Available at http://www.ssrc.org/sept11/essays/wallerstein.htm.

Williams, W. Appleman. *Empire as a Way of Life.* New York: Oxford University Press, 1980.

——. *A William Appleman Williams Reader,* edited by Henry Berger. Chicago: Ivan R. Dee, 1992.

Wood, Ellen. "Contradictions: Only in Capitalism?" In *The Socialist Register* (2002): 275–93. London and New York: Monthly Review Press, 2002.

# index

index   135

**Paul Smith** is professor of cultural studies at George Mason University. He is author of *Discerning the Subject* and *Clint Eastwood: A Cultural Production*, both published by the University of Minnesota Press.